THE ENERGY HEALERS
ORACLE
TOOLS FOR TOTAL TRANSFORMATION
VOLUME II

ANGELA ORORA MEDWAY-SMITH

FEATURING: CHRYSTAL ROSE ADDISON, KIMBERLY BARRETT, ANITA D. DAVIES, DebS,
CAROLYN NICHOLSON FOWLER, ANNE GORDON, STEPHANIE JONES, STEFANIE KERNLER,
KWALI KUMARA, TOVE KIRSTY LEWIS, DR. HEIDI M. MACALPINE, CAROLINE MARY,
JOAN OSBORNE, JENNIFER PALMER, SOFIA PEREIRA, ANGELINE POON,
DIANA SAVIL, AMANDA SLADE, NYDIA LAYSA STONE, LAINIE SEVANTE WULKAN

THE ENERGY HEALER'S

ORACLE

TOOLS FOR TOTAL TRANSFORMATION

VOLUME II

ANGELA ORORA MEDWAY-SMITH

FEATURING: CHRYSTAL ROSE ADDISON, KIMBERLY BARRETT, ANITA D. DAVIES, DebS, CAROLYN NICHOLSON FOWLER, ANNE GORDON, STEPHANIE JONES, STEFANIE KERNLER, KWALI KUMARA, TOVE KIRSTY LEWIS, DR. HEIDI M. MACALPINE, CAROLINE MARY, JOAN OSBORNE, JENNIFER PALMER, SOFIA PEREIRA, ANGELINE POON, DIANA SAVIL, AMANDA SLADE, NYDIA LAYSA STONE, LAINIE SEVANTE WULKAN

The Energy Healer's Oracle Volume II

Tools for Total Transformation

Angela Orora Medway-Smith

Copyright ©2024 Angela Orora Medway-Smith

Published by Brave Healer Productions

Print ISBN: 978-1-961493-35-3

eBook ISBN: 978-1-961493-34-6

WHAT THEY SAY

"The Energy Healer's Oracle—Tools for Total Transformation by Angela Orora Medway-Smith is an invaluable treasure trove of deep mystical and practical wisdom that you can easily incorporate into your busy life.

Powerful accounts shared by a distinguished group of mystics and healers reveal their profound lifetime knowledge. This is a book you will want to keep by your side."

Itzhak Beery, Ancestral medicine teacher, healer, speaker, and author of The Gift of Shamanism, Shamanic Transformations, and Shamanic Healing. https://www.itzhakbeery.com/

* * *

"Clear a space on your table for the most impactful healing book you'll ever read! You'll find yourself unable to put this book down as you race to the next chapter of amazing real-life stories and healing tools. Friends, family, and even strangers you bless should brace themselves for their miraculous recoveries and inexplicable healing simply because you read THIS book."

Amy Gillespie Dougherty, Author of "The Ancestors Within" book series, host of "The Eyes Have it! Unlocking your Ancestral Code with Amy" on Ethereal television network. www.illuminationstation.org

* * *

"There are many different modalities of healing around the world. The Huichol way of healing is to integrate healing of the person, the community and our Mother Earth. This book captures the essence of healing and offers various tools and techniques. It is a guidebook that can help many people discover what works for them on their own healing journey."

Brant Secunda, Healer & Shaman in the Huichol tradition and founder of the Dance of the Deer Foundation, Center for Shamanic Studies. https://www.shamanism.com

* * *

"I have been an admirer of Angela for many years. She is one spiritual, talented lady. I thoroughly enjoyed Angela's straight forward style of writing, detailing her life and achievements with her spiritual, and healing gifts. I enjoyed her attention to detail with the tools and practices which she used with her healing work.

The wonderful healing modalities of other experts are also included in this book with their fascinating life journeys.

This book will be a beacon of light, hope for countless people, to help transform life challenges, with practical steps, advice, and inspirational guidance; proving healing energy is accessible to everyone.

Lesley Ball, International Medium, Usui Reiki Master and Divine Channel. https://www.facebook.com/lesley.ball.902

* * *

"'Inspirational' is the overwhelming feeling resonating from the pages of this, the second volume of The Energy Healer' Oracle. What sets this book apart is its introduction of new modalities for healing, a common thread among the twenty-one contributors.

Each chapter, written by an expert in the modality, offers a unique perspective. The book is not just well written but a pleasure to read.

One interesting phenomena is the domino effect of a desire to heal through self-discovery leading to creating tools to heal others. "Ask and you will receive", "Feel pain of mind, body and spirit", and we will receive, these are just some of the themes coursing through the pages.

All authors are specialists in their field and offer tools to the reader/seeker enabling a gentle introduction to the modality, and a birthing of partnership with the energies and intelligence vibrating through our multidimensional universe.

'Hell on earth became my heaven on earth'; is a grand mantra for self-healing and helps us to understand the need to flip negatives, i.e. dis-ease, into positives- wellness of mind, body and spirit; "Be like a tree, firm no matter what", a mantra for perseverance, and the importance of grounding in everything.

This book is packed with sound, tried, and tested guidance, and none of the tools offered are difficult, as many are guided imagery akin to self-hypnosis techniques to invoke deep relaxation, focus, direction, and resolution of dis-ease and connect with the divine. The common thread throughout is breath and appropriate controls thereof, as one should in any meditative practice.

Reading the personal stories of each author enables us to understand the whys and, like all explorers of growth and connection, leads the reader to hitherto undiscovered shores.

One can take many adventures with this book, the challenge is, which journey will you sign up for after experiencing the 'taster tools', no matter, your map for self-discovery will be found within these pages with an array of global links.

'Breathe and Be'"

Lazarus Carpenter, Curative Hypnotherapist, Psychotherapist, Trance Channel, Broadcaster, and award-winning author has channelled Edgar Cayce since 1992. He has worked extensively with energy healing in various forms including pyramids and crystals; recently, he completed an 18-month research project channelling the energies of Craig y Nos Castle in Wales, the former home of opera diva, Adelina Patti. Volume One of his work, 'Walls Have Ears' is now available, as is the television series, Whisperings of Craig Y Nos, based on his books. https://lazaruscarpenterauthor.com

This book is dedicated to my darling husband Ian, my soul mate, my rock, and our beautiful children.

Thank you for choosing to walk through the journey of this life with me.

My love for you knows no bounds.

DISCLAIMER

This book offers health and nutritional information and is designed for educational purposes only. You should not rely on this information as a substitute for, nor does it replace professional medical advice, diagnosis, or treatment. If you have any concerns or questions about your health, you should always consult with a physician or other healthcare professional. Do not disregard, avoid, or delay obtaining medical or health-related advice from your healthcare professional because of something you may have read here. The use of any information provided in this book is solely at your own risk.

Developments in medical research may impact the health, fitness, and nutritional advice that appears here. No assurances can be given that the information contained in this book will always include the most relevant findings or developments with respect to the particular material.

Having said all that, know that the experts here have shared their tools, practices, and knowledge with you with a sincere and generous intent to assist you on your health and wellness journey. Please contact them with any questions you may have about the techniques or information they provided. They will be happy to assist you further!

FOREWORD

The Energy Healer's Oracle takes the reader on a fascinating journey of discovery into the occult world of mysticism, mediumship, spirituality, and energy healing.

This is a 'must read' for newcomers eager to understand their path and purpose in life as well as for 'old souls' who will recognise and re-discover many of the healing journeys and topics covered.

This wonderful book is much needed for our troubled world that is crying out for guidance and healing. It aligns beautifully with my vision for the Peace Mala educational project, which I began in the dark days following the terrible events of 9/11 – a day that changed our world forever. September 11th, 2001, brought with it an aftermath of fear and confusion that sadly persists.

The news constantly reminds us that we are living in very troubled times. I'm sure that many of us often wake in the morning with heavy hearts. All the more reason, therefore, to do the little acts of kindness and healing each one of us is capable of.

There isn't a soul on this planet who has not experienced times of sorrow, ill-health, fear or despair. During such times, it is the kind word, the healing touch, and the support of others that can bring us back into balance. By reaching out to one another with true compassion and indiscriminate loving kindness, we can heal each other and our world.

Hope is what we must all hang on to, with faith and trust that even in the midst of great darkness and fear, good will always prevail. Unconditional love is the key to happiness and healing in our lives.

The Energy Healer's Oracle shares remarkable spiritual and healing experiences. It reminds us that with love and trust, there is a way of recovering from whatever trauma, tragedy, or illness we may encounter in our lives.

This is a book that shares profound spiritual insights into how there is far more to life than what may appear as 'the ordinary.' As we grow spiritually, we learn that love is what connects us and opens up the pathway to peace, harmony, and healing.

Deep congratulations to Angela Orora Medway-Smith, and all who have contributed their amazing life experiences on the spiritual path.

Pam Evans MBE
Author, Master Teacher of Usui Reiki and Seichem Healing
Founder of the multi award-winning Peace Mala educational project for world peace

www.peacemala.org.uk

Registered Charity No. 1118053

Endorsed by His Holiness Pope Francis, His Holiness The Dalai Lama of Tibet and Archbishop Emeritus Desmond Tutu

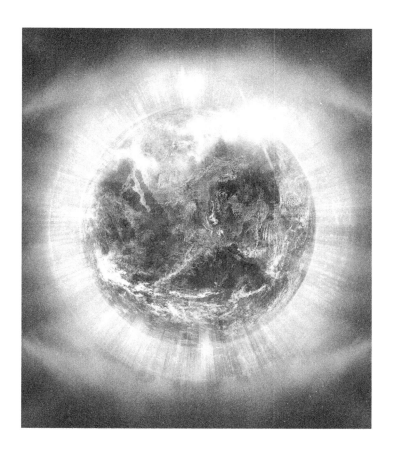

Jennifer Hawkyard is a multidisciplinary artist and designer living and working in remote West Wales. She specializes in creating intuitively led channeled artwork and messages for her clientele all over the world. Her work is multi-dimensional, colorful, and imbued with layers of insight, love, and significance.

Connect with Jennifer:

Website: www.jezhawk.com

Facebook: https://www.facebook.com/jezhawk/

Instagram: https://www.instagram.com/jezhawk/

Etsy: etsy.com/uk/shop/JezhawkUK

Twitter: https://twitter.com/jezhawk

TABLE OF CONTENTS

INTRODUCTION

"Everything is energy, and that's all there is to it. Match the frequency of the reality you want, and you cannot help but get that reality. It can be no other way. This is not philosophy. This is physics."

~ Albert Einstein

Welcome to *The Energy Healer's Oracle*, where we dive into the electrifying world of energy healing! Imagine a universe where everything dances to its own beat, from the tiniest molecules to your spirit's wildest dreams.

In today's fast-paced world, we're all being bombarded by energy frequencies, influenced by vibrations that shape our being; our mind, body, spirit, and soul.

As an energy healer for almost four decades, I've seen the magic unfold in this realm. With a treasure trove of healing techniques now at our fingertips, we're riding the wave of new energy healing modalities and holistic therapies that complement modern medicine.

But with so many paths to choose from, it's easy to feel a bit lost in the energy maze. That's where this book comes in!

It's your ticket to exploring high-vibrational energy healing methods, meeting the master teachers, and tapping into new modalities straight from Source.

From ancient traditions to modern-day miracles, energy frequencies can spin your world around. Get ready for a toolkit filled with wisdom from the planet's leading healers, designed to sprinkle a dash of magic on your holistic wellness journey.

Throughout history, healers from all corners of the globe have harnessed the power of energies to weave healing miracles. Many powerful ancient traditions have been retained, particularly those of shamanic traditions of the indigenous peoples the world over.

Fast forward to the 20th century, when channels tapped into healing frequencies like Usui Reiki Ryoho, paving the way for a healing revolution.

This revolution has blossomed into a garden of healing schools and techniques. Our book shines a light on divine channels sharing fresh, high-vibrational modalities channeled straight from the cosmic source as well as those better-known frequencies and ancient techniques.

Whether it's Reiki or any other healing practice, the common thread is the healer becoming a vessel for divine energy to flow, bringing harmony and wellness to those in need.

Healers are like energy DJs, spinning healing frequencies through their hands and hearts, guided by intuition and a treasure trove of tools to perfectly match each client's needs, guided by connection with divine energy.

This book is an Oracle, a collection of wisdom from seasoned master healers, each sharing a glimpse into transformative wellness journeys and powerful healing tools.

As you flip through the pages, let this Oracle guide you into the enchanting world of energy healing, unlocking the secrets to your transformative future.

So, dear reader, as Einstein also said, "The medicine of the future will be the medicine of frequencies."

Your healing journey starts here and now.

What are you waiting for?

Wishing you boundless blessings and radiant transformations,

Angela Orora Medway-Smith

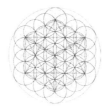

CHAPTER 1

SPIRITUAL HEALING

FIND YOUR SOUL'S PATH
WITH MANKIND'S ORIGINAL THERAPY

Angela Orora Medway-Smith, The Practical Mystic

MY STORY

What in God's name is happening?

I immersed my hands in water which began to bubble and fizz. Incredulous, I stared at my reflection in the mirror above the sink.

The face that looked back at me was not mine.

I blinked.

This time, my face, but my whole body glowed and shimmered.

What the hell?

I looked down. The water had stopped bubbling. I steadied myself, dried my hands, and returned to my tarot reading class; it was the first session.

I pulled the teacher to one side and told her what happened. She looked terrified.

"I think you need my teacher; she can help you understand what just happened," Nomi said shakily. She scribbled a phone number down on a slip of paper and thrust it into my hand.

The class continued, and I found it hard to concentrate; soon, I was walking from the tiny Victorian tenement along the freezing cold South London street towards the tube station. A gang of youths lounged against a shiny red London phone box, music pounded from their boombox; they leered and catcalled to me.

Head down, I huddled into my coat and walked faster, reaching the safety of the station. Descending the escalator, the heat from the tunnels hit me.

Sitting quietly, safely on the train, eyes closed, I began to process my experience as we rumbled noisily from station to station.

Suddenly, a wave of pain hit me like a steamroller.

My leg? Oh my God, what's happening to me?

It came from nowhere.

I breathed deeply to calm the pain and opened my eyes.

Sitting opposite me was a man who just got on, his leg in plaster, clutching his crutches, his face contorted in pain.

It's not my pain, it's his! How can this be happening?

My stop was next. I leapt from my seat, almost running.

Soon, I was sitting on my bed staring at the phone number and name on the slip of paper: Betty Balcombe.

I had to phone in the morning.

I had to understand what was happening.

"I've been waiting for your call," said Betty. "Come to my home next week. You can join the healers who can't make my Hampstead class."

"Sorry, healers?" I said. "Did Nomi tell you she'd given me your number?"

"Yes my dear you're a healer, you've been sent to me to remember. No, I've been waiting for you to call for a while. You'll be fine until Wednesday. I'll see you then."

The receiver clicked as Betty put down the phone. I sat dumbfounded listening to the sound of the line droning as my mind raced.

I'm a healer?

She knew I was going to call?

I'd be fine?

I'm a very practical person. I've always been a pragmatist. At this point, I was a sensible young woman aged 22.

When I was a child, I had imaginary friends and was able to intuit what was going to happen, to sense the energy before I entered a room. I hid in my books, my safe space, and blocked out anything that prevented me not being able to fit in.

This was way beyond my comfort zone!

Hiding in my books once more, I avoided the trains and used buses instead for the next week until it was time to meet Betty.

I knocked on the door of the neat suburban semi. Looking down, I noticed the gleaming step. There was a chill in the air.

A glowing, willowy woman with huge dark eyes and a beaming smile greeted me.

"Come in, Angela!" she smiled and held out her arms to hug me.

I was home.

A home I hadn't remembered, reconnecting with the divine soul who agreed to help me remember who I am.

For the next seven years, Wednesday evenings at Betty's were my haven from the world.

It was my secret space where I truly belonged, rediscovering the tools, techniques, and many lives I spent as a healer and mystic—lives in ancient civilizations where I served as a seer, oracle, priest, priestess, wise woman, hedge-witch, myrrophore and shaman. I was one of 'Betty's people.'

I started working part-time as a spiritual healer and psychic, and in 1990 traveled to Australia, teaching Betty's course. I later came to this work full-time, deeply embedded on my soul's path, eternally grateful for my beloved teacher.

Many years later, I helped start a healing evening at my local spiritualist church and looked forward to serving spirit and my community every week.

"How are you feeling now?" I asked my client at the end of our session.

Susan had been coming for a few months and asked for me to work with her every Monday evening.

"Wonderful! I was only thinking this morning how different my life is since I've been coming here. I have less pain and more mobility, I'm eating better and now look forward to getting up in the morning. It feels like I've left a very dark place in my life. I can't thank you enough," she said.

"That's brilliant. I'm so pleased, but it's not me, I'm simply the channel, Susan. The healing energy is channeled from the Divine, and I'm supported by angels and guides in the spirit world who know where to direct it. You were ready to change your life, otherwise you wouldn't be here. Every week we've been chipping away at the layers of disharmony you gathered. I've been starting to see you shine for a while." I smiled warmly.

My life also changed, my guides were encouraging me to teach once more.

"It's so frustrating!" I said to my husband. "My guides are clear. They want me to teach. I've booked the venue and scheduled 22 classes, but when I sit down at the computer to complete the lesson plan I get nothing! It's been a week, and I still don't know where to start. I'm going to take a day off tomorrow and maybe go to Lesley's meditation group, see if that helps."

He nodded in support without looking away from the television, "Sounds like a plan."

It'd been two years since I started my spiritual business. My business evolved from working as a healer and clairvoyant locally to organizing charity festivals, fairs, and spiritual events, and then to making the 400-mile round trip to London fortnightly to work as a spiritual consultant at Mysteries, the world-famous esoteric book shop in London's Covent Garden.

The following morning, I headed out to the local community center, set in the middle of a leafy park. I stopped for a moment, breathed deeply, and listened to the birdsong and the stream tinkling gently nearby before heading inside the modern red brick building.

A circle of chairs was laid out in front of a long table with candles and crystals. The smell of incense hung in the air. I smiled from the heart. I loved Lesley's circles; they were so welcoming. Laughter rang from the kitchen. I dropped my coat and bag on a chair and headed in to join the friendly group making tea.

The routine was the same every week—a guided meditation and then some mediumship or psychic development. Most of the lovely people who came didn't really need the practice; it was just a place to gather with friends. I didn't come very often, but was usually led here when I needed to listen or be given a message.

So, it wasn't a big surprise when close to the end of the morning when one of the ladies said, "Angela, your grandfather is here, he has a message for you."

She went on to describe my grandfather, a gentle giant of a man who rarely steps back into this world unless it's important.

"He says, step away from the computer, what you need is on the bookshelf," she continued excitedly.

"And soon, your training courses will have accreditation, you'll be teaching all over the world! He's very proud of what you're going to achieve," she said with a beaming smile.

I thanked her, smiling in disbelief.

How can what I need be already done? My home is filled with bookshelves. Would I need to look through every book? There's absolutely no way I'd be putting myself through accrediting my own courses. Way too much work!

My grandfather took the trouble to bring me the message, so I needed to look at least.

An hour later, I opened a dusty envelope that miraculously found its way to the bookshelf in my living room.

Inside was a typed lesson plan for a 22-week intuitive development course. My wonderful Betty gave me the envelope and its contents thirty years earlier.

I still have no idea how it came to be there. I moved my home six times, and every other book on the shelf was under ten years old!

I firmly believe that if our soul's plan includes something we need to do, we will be provided with the means to do it.

On the first week of my Spiritual Development Course, students learned and practiced psychometry (the reading of photographs or objects); during the sixth week, they'd be challenged to read photographs inside sealed envelopes to show them how far they'd developed.

"Write some notes and tell me what you've picked up," I said to my class.

We moved around the room one by one as the students described colors, shapes, feelings, and images they'd picked up, holding the sealed envelopes and then opening them in amazement to find they'd tuned into the energy of a place or person, picked up the color of clothing, the shape of a mountain, or the bends of a river in the pictures inside.

"I've drawn a picture," said Ann.

"The more I tune in, the stronger it gets. It's as if I'm watching a video. I'm seeing a young woman in a purple robe holding a chalice. She's a Priestess I think? She's with a small entourage, and I can see the pyramids. They're in Egypt."

"What do you feel?" I asked.

"A deep sense of service, of contentment," she added.

"Okay, let's open the envelope, you may have picked up on a past life of one of the people in the picture," I said.

Ann opened the envelope, and my jaw literally hit the floor as she pulled out a school photograph of me, aged 7.

She handed me the drawing, "You need to keep this and ask your guides why they're showing you this." She smiled.

Later, at home, I sat in meditation with sacred oils. I'd started 'myrrophore work', meditating with individual oils to learn from them and tune into their sacred vibrations. Some brought forward ancient symbols, images, and messages. I hadn't worked with Myrtle before but was guided to select it.

I inhaled the scent deeply, closed my eyes, and relaxed. The scent brought more smells forward, and sounds and images started to play as I was transported back to the same life that Ann had seen earlier.

"Lie down and relax, sister; I'll fetch us some water," I said, as my companion made herself comfortable on a lumpy-looking mattress on a low wooden bed. I looked around the room.

It was hot and dusty; we were both heavily pregnant, plaster peeled off the walls, and I could see the rough stone underneath.

I waddled to the next room; several men were huddled on stools around a wooden table; I was handed a clay jug and a drinking vessel and returned to my friend; she smiled at me as we drank thirstily. My name was Mary, and my companion was Mary Magdalene; we were in Egypt. The image faded.

What does this mean? Why am I being shown this? I don't understand. I quizzed my guides.

Follow the signs and listen.

Later that same day, I was checking my e-mails when my tablet froze. Unable to scroll back or forward, I paid attention to the message. The College of Psychic Studies in London was running a workshop four days later; "Receive the Keys to the Pyramid," it read.

I turned to my husband, "Darling, I'm going to London on Friday, there's a course I need to be on."

The initiations I received at that workshop reawakened my ability to channel ascended masters and angels. The ascended master St. Germain became a regular visitor to my development group, and my connection to my guides, beings of light, and my higher self (my soul) became crystal clear.

I continued teaching, moving my focus to teaching healing.

The world needs healers to help with what will come, said St. Germain in 2019.

Today, I teach many energy-healing systems, some of which you will read about in this book.

As I explained to Susan, we healers are all simply channels for the Divine supported by angels, spirit guides, ascended masters, ancestors, and sometimes galactic healers, all in light form.

Everyone can channel healing energy.

The wonderful thing is when you send healing to others you also receive residual energy; it can be quite addictive!

The tool I'll be sharing with you today is a simple technique that I used to teach my spiritual development class as an introduction to channeling healing energy.

THE TOOL

Before You Begin

Spiritual or psychic protection is an essential first step before beginning any healing or spiritual practice. This was the step missed by my first spiritual teacher which caused me so much discomfort.

It's not complicated and simply involves requesting protection from higher powers. Here's a simple prayer:

Simple Daily Protection

Divine Spirit, Creator of All,

I call forth now my guides and ministering angels,

to draw close, to bring me guidance and protection,

now, and until I leave this earthly realm.

Amen

THE PRACTICE

First, relax. Use your breath to relax deeply, and move this relaxation through your body through the energy centers (chakras).

Cleanse, clear, relax, release, heal, and harmonize your body, and shift any negative or stuck energy in the subtle energy body.

Take at least two breaths at each chakra, and be intuitive. If you need to release more tension or stuck energy, then repeat.

It's helpful to visualize your chakras as Catherine Wheels, seeing sparks of stuck energy drifting away to be grounded into Mother Earth, to be repurposed, recycled, and reborn.

Make your body comfortable, roll back your shoulders, and gently move your neck to release any tension. Make sure that your arms and legs are uncrossed, and if sitting, connect your feet with the floor beneath you.

Breathe deeply. In through your nose, and out through your mouth, deep into your lungs. For a moment, simply be aware of the rise and fall of your belly.

Turn your attention to the person (your client) you're sending healing to and set a clear intention by saying:

"I ask for healing for the highest good of all and harm of none for (name), in accordance with the will of the Divine and the will of the higher self."

Next:

Imagine you're seated on a chair opposite your client

You are now a channel for the divine.

Don't worry about getting it wrong; there are higher powers in charge of this; you're simply the channel.

Visualize a laser beam of neon green light emanating from the center of your forehead, your third eye.

The light travels to a point above the head of your client and is wider than their body.

With your intention, slowly move this laser beam of divine light down their body to their feet, pausing when you feel you need to, being intuitive, taking your time.

Repeat this process as often as you feel you need to.

When you feel it's time to finish give thanks to all of the beings of light that have supported you.

Ground yourself by breathing some energy into your root chakra, sending some energetic roots into the Earth to ground and steady yourself, call in your usual spiritual protection, and take a drink of water.

If you're new to channeling energy, just try five to ten minutes and build up to fifteen to twenty.

You can also use this technique for yourself, imagining the neon green light tube moving down your own body. It's a great way to unwind at the end of the day and prepare for a restful night's sleep.

Remember to take great care when transitioning from spiritual work back into the everyday world. It's essential to ground, center, and reset your energy system to a safe operating level. I tell my students to think of it like hitting the standby button on their TVs. Ensure that you're properly grounded, particularly before driving.

In these pages, and our previous volume, you'll find information and inspiration on many different therapies and frequencies of energy healing.

We live in a world where we're remembering how our ancestors healed and have access to literally hundreds of options for our own healing journey.

If you're interested in finding out more about my work with the ascended master and archangelic realms, check out my channeled books and oracle cards, Alchemical Aura Mists, recorded meditations, and courses; I also offer spiritual consultations, Life & Soul Alignment Coaching, healer training, and mentoring; check out my website: https://www.cariadspiritual.com.

I also teach accredited healing courses on retreats in sacred places around our beautiful planet.

Find out more here:

https://www.cariadspiritual.com/retreat-priority-list

As a thank you for purchasing this book, you can pick up a free downloadable meditation to meet your guardian angel and spirit guides, beings who can support you with your healing practice and spiritual development:

https://www.cariadspiritual.com/oracle-volume2-gift

Allowing yourself to be a channel for divine energy is a precious divine gift.

Working with spiritual healing energy can truly transform your being, and align you to your soul's path.

I hope you feel inspired.

Angela Orora Medway-Smith, "The Practical Mystic," is a Welsh spiritual channel and teacher, master healer, coach, and retreat leader. Her business is called Cariad Spiritual, and she works both in person and online, spreading the light at workshops, festivals, conferences, and retreats worldwide.

Holistic healing is Angela's passion. She's Chair of a non-profit, Divine Energy International, dedicated to promoting energy healing and supporting healers of various modalities.

She's set up healing clinics, created charity holistic events and festivals, and trained and supported thousands of individuals worldwide with healing and guidance from spirit.

She devotes her life to awakening divine souls like you to their potential. She believes that we all can transform, emerge from the chrysalis of this human life, 'be the butterfly,' and soar, reclaiming our sovereign self, developing a deep connection to our soul, and aligning with our true destiny.

Angela is incredibly blessed to be a direct channel for the Ascended Master and Angelic Realms. She has published two channeled books: *The Book of Many Colours: Awaken Your Soul's Purpose With The Divine Rays* and *The Book of Many Flames: Everyday Alchemy With Esoteric Energy*.

She's also co-author of six #1 international Amazon best-selling books on holistic healing, which you can find here:

https://www.amazon.co.uk/stores/Angela-Orora-Medway-Smith/author/B09L5X6T7X

Angela offers spiritual consultations, coaching, mentoring, retreats, healing, healer, and intuitive development training worldwide.

She loves to empower others to kick-start their healing journey and spiritual development.

When she's not supporting others or with her family, you'll find Angela by water, walking along the banks of the Thames, which flows near her London home, or along the beach close to her hometown in Wales.

Connect with Angela at: https://linktr.ee/angela_orora_medwaysmith

Remember to sign up for her newsletter to receive monthly gifts and news.

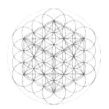

CHAPTER 2

LABYRINTH ACTIVATION FOR TRANSFORMING GRIEF

TRANSITIONING THE HEART FROM ANGUISH TO ACCEPTANCE

Lainie Sevante Wulkan, 4th Generation Multi-Modality Healer

"With a labyrinth, you make a choice to go in - and once you've chosen, around and around you go.
But you always find your way to the center."

~ Jeff Bridges

MY STORY

They were supposed to be here. Why, dear God, did they have to die? This was our girls' trip, our getaway to paradise.

Sometimes life doesn't give you a choice, but rather, the universe makes one for you. This was one of those times. One of my best girlfriends, Heather, was dying of cancer. She took a turn for the worse. There was an evident change of energy in the air. I felt it down to my core. My stomach went from butterflies to knots of steel, and a wave of sadness, deep, gut-wrenching sadness, crept in. While on our weekly phone calls, instead of planning all the fun we were looking forward to on our Costa Rica retreat, the tone turned further into realistic conversations about her near future. We weren't going to be eating five-star food, exploring the lush jungle for monkeys and sloths, and dancing like school kids under a cascading waterfall. We were gearing up for a funeral. Poof! A ten-year friendship I leaned on was gone, a support system seemingly ripped away in the blink of an eye. I was shattered.

And then it happened again, like lightning striking the same tree. Jenee suddenly passed.

Oh no, this can't be true! Not Jenee too.

A few months before the retreat, Jenee, one of my gal pals and fellow yoginis, joined my yoga teacher, Patti, and me on a three-day jaunt to the desert for "Bhaktifest," a spiritual music yoga festival nestled in the heart of Joshua Tree, California. The stars were not only aligned for this "sojourn into bliss" but sparkled in the millions above our heads in the sky as we danced the night away to our favorite musical artists such as Michael Franti and MC Yogi (in the front row, no less). Everything was aligned. Grown women squealing like teenagers on spring break. Three days of girl talk, hanging out in Jenee's RV, enjoying yoga classes, music, and spiritual workshops. We were on top of the world and talked incessantly about how much fun we're going to have in Costa Rica in just a couple of months. The big trip was almost here after planning the retreat for so long. It was so close and real. We felt its ocean breeze and salty air at that very moment, which was such a sharp contrast to the stark, scalding hot desert we were currently in. The next yoga-music-jungle experience was nearly imminent. Or so I thought.

"I don't know how to tell you this, but Jenee passed away last night," I listened with complete shock from her husband's voicemail. We'd barely been home a week. I was stopped in my tracks and absolutely crushed.

No, no, no! This can't be true. Absolutely not! We just laughed our hearts out in the desert and planned future adventures. Not again! Spirit, I give up. I can't take this!

As a lifelong multi-modality energy healer, wellness coach, spiritual teacher, mystic, and oracle, I'm usually the one doing the healing for others. Costa Rica was my spiritual retreat. I had coordinated for everyone: clients, family, and friends. Nourish Your Soul Retreats™—this was a plan in the making for over a year. Every meticulous detail was thought of, from the cacao ceremonies and sound healing to medicinal herb tours and plant-based cooking classes. Every five-star meal was thought of and created with great intention, aligning with the elements of nature. As excited as the time was approaching to finally get going, I was still coping with reality—two of my girlfriends wouldn't be there to enjoy it all and see the hard work and efforts pay off, at least in physical form.

It's here as I imagined. Our Costa Rican Nourish Your Soul Retreat™ was happening. Every day was an honoring of the senses. Mother Gaia, and her beautiful elements of earth, air, fire, water, and spirit. It was day five—Spirit Day, and the culminating activity for this beautiful group of 26 women was about to unfold. The finale of a week of renewal, restoration, expansion, and transformation was here. We were about to experience a shamanic practice I was certain the group hadn't experienced before—a labyrinth walk on the beach. This was a special labyrinth being built in front of our eyes. Expertly hand-crafted with energetic care and with a simple rake, the shaman designed a magnificent healing tool and pulled from the energies of the group. I've walked labyrinths all over the world in a variety of settings with structures built from an array of natural materials, and even I had never seen anything like it before. My excitement mounted, and my vow to work through my grief was ever so present.

Girls, thank you for being with me all week. I felt your presence greatly and feel you in my heart right now.

During the retreat's experiences, when I let go of what feelings no longer served me in the waterfall and fire ceremonies, they were there. When I ate white bean croquettes over grilled chilotes with pumpkin puree or carrot, green onion, and ginger cream soup, or any of the incredible meals and healthy drinks from the unlimited wellness bar, they were there. Both of these ladies, like me, were foodies. They would've loved it. I ate, drank, walked, laughed, meditated, and prayed in their honor.

I feel your Spirits here, ladies. Let's walk together this labyrinth and rejoice in the time we had together and the memories forever etched in my heart.

"Safe Travels," said the sign, hand-drawn in the sand as we entered this mystical maze of enlightenment. I smiled and felt a warmth of energy run through my heart. What a great way to start my walk with mindfulness, intention, and change. Labyrinths do that. They beckon transformational healing. After all, they're ancient archetypes and sacred symbols known in a variety of cultures for eons.

Walking through this labyrinth had a purpose. The culmination of the emotions I felt over the week was extensive. Being "on" for the group and giving my love and devotion to their well-being was both rewarding and, at times, heavy, as I had moments of anger, anguish, sadness, and exhaustion to deal with. I needed to nourish my soul and find a sense of peace with the passing of my friends. I needed to return to joy.

Okay Spirit. I'm ready to heal and find my way back to center. Let the labyrinth show me the way.

As I took a deep breath, said a short prayer, and set an intention, I took my first steps inside the maze. As I found my gait and steadied my pace, I immediately began to feel supported and joined by an energy that felt otherworldly. I was not alone.

As I walked around the spirals, I noticed my feelings of grief lifted with ease, and the transition from anguish to acceptance came into clear view. As I made it to the center, I stopped, smiled, and expressed gratitude to the universe for arriving better than when I started. I knew I was already at a new level of freedom from my emotional pain.

On my walk out, I continued to feel energy being released back to Mother Nature into the glistening, sun-kissed ocean, waiting to wash away my tears. A transmutation occurred, and I felt a renewed sense of self.

Whew. Thank you, God. Bless you, friends.

The retreat was over, and the journey home began. I experienced so many reflections on what transpired in Costa Rica. I felt more love in my heart and profound memories emblazoned in my soul. It was a success for so many reasons, both personally and professionally. My cup was full.

Heather and Jenee are a part of me, along with other angels who have untimely transitioned from my life before. Now, they're my guides and spirit protectors, giving me the inspiration to go on and be a beacon of light for others during their times of darkness. I'm grateful that the right healing tools, activities, and processes showed up for me when I needed them most. The labyrinth is one of those powerful processes I love so dearly. It affords me a reminder of patience and stillness in this fast-paced world. It offers a moment to slow down and appreciate what I have for as long as I have it. I wish the same for you. Namaste.

THE TOOL

I weave my own experiences of working with a labyrinth, along with professional spiritual training to help you with loss. I understand, have been there, and am a pillar of support when the road gets rocky. Let the energy of labyrinth healing be a steady guide towards your own heart of healing and navigate a path home.

Where to Begin

A physical, walking labyrinth is usually found at spiritual or retreat centers, churches or as part of a group activity created specifically with intentions. Consider looking up where the closest labyrinth is in your area at my FB group, Labyrinth Love, https://bit.ly/LabryrinthLove. Our loving group has samples of many labyrinths and stories of hope and healing.

Make Your Own

If you can't find one, make one. You can look online and find templates to create either indoor or outdoor designs. There are even labyrinth mats that can be purchased and used.

Finger Labyrinth

One of my favorite labyrinths can be done without leaving the comfort of your home. If you have a meditation area or altar, consider printing out a small labyrinth on a piece of paper from resources online. Some stencils can be downloaded to draw your own as well. As they say, "Let your fingers do the walking." One of my favorite labyrinth card sets can be found here:

https://amzn.to/3UeBJYk

For now and in this moment, I invite you to envision a labyrinth in your mind. Enjoy the ride below.

MIND LABYRINTH FOR TRANSFORMING GRIEF - LET'S ACTIVATE AND HEAL

Set your space. Light a candle, put on some soft instrumental music, and perhaps burn some incense or a put few drops of essential oil into a diffuser. Align your energies to the room.

Take this time to quiet your being and allow your heart to be present. Give yourself the freedom to disconnect from the outer world, close your eyes, and go inside.

Begin with deep, slow, steady breaths. See the color green breathing in and out of your heart. Do this three times. Set the intention to heal. Your heart chakra is energizing.

Bring your attention to your third eye (forehead center between your eyebrows). See the color indigo. Feel the energy here moving, spinning in a clockwise direction, opening wider to the portal to your soul.

Think of a person you've loved and lost and bring them to your mind's eye. Say hello. Invite them to be with you now on your labyrinth walk.

Feel their presence with your senses. Allow this mindful journey to unfold the messages you'd like to hear. Choose to be okay—because you are.

Next, imagine a mandala or labyrinth that has a beginning entry that spirals towards a center. See your loved one walking with you. Notice where they are. Do you see them walking in front of you, beside or behind? Are they in physical form or more ethereal and angelic? However you see them, it is perfect. Notice as you walk to the center if they have any messages for you. Do you have questions for them? Ask them to heal your pain; ask them to lighten your suffering.

Keep walking slowly in your mind towards the center. Allow any burdened energy to release as you forgive yourself for any judgments you might have placed on yourself, them, or others. See yourself more buoyant as you make it to the center.

Once there, stop for a moment. What do you hear, smell, taste, or feel? Breathe. Once again, breathe the healing energy of green in and out. Allow your out-breath to be more pronounced, even invoke a sound if you care to. Let it all out, loud and proud. You've been through a lot! Let your grief escape!

Continue on the spiral, now following its path slowly out of the maze. What is happening inside? How are you feeling? You may find that as you depart the center your loved one isn't there anymore. They've gracefully moved into their world as you begin to move stronger and steadier in yours. While they might not be there in physical form, they are still standing beside you, in front and behind. Know this to be true. Feel the support you have as you walk your way home.

As you finally begin your exit, give yourself the gift of acceptance. Everything is perfect, Divine, and aligned. Accept you are walking your path perfectly for you and you will be led and nourished with what you need. You'll also soon see that all you ever need is already inside. The answers are already there. So are your loved ones. Anytime you need them, just tap into your heart space and call their name.

When you're complete with your labyrinth walk, slowly bring yourself back to the room and into your body. Stretch your arms and legs. Open your eyes.

You may want to journal your reflections on your experience of your labyrinth walk.

I wish you safe travels on your journey and wholeheartedly invite you to join me for a live, in-person experience. Let's walk the labyrinth of wellness together. It would be my honor to have you join me for our heart-opening, mind-warming, epic, healing transformations on our Nourish Your Soul Retreats™. More wellness awaits in paradise. I hope to see you soon, either there or with a private healing. You deserve it.

All my love,

Sevante

Lainie Sevante is a fourth-generation intuitive healer. She's the founder of The Center for Intuitive Food Therapy (CIFT), Nourish Your Soul Ayurveda, and Nourish Your Soul Retreats. She's a multi-modality healer with advanced certifications in food healing, theta healing, tuning Forks, EFT/tapping, and the Law of Attraction. She holds a BS in food science, dietetics, and nutrition. She's the international bestselling author of *The Food Healing Oracle Deck – Nourishing Wisdom from Mother Earth* (Co-Authored Vol. 1 and 2), which is read in 35 countries, and is currently writing Volume 3; She wrote the revised *Smoothies – Nourishing Wisdom Beyond the Blend*, #1 Amazon bestselling, *Top Exotic Foods for Natural Healing* and wrote Chapter 3 for *The Energy Healers Oracle 1*. Sevante is now writing the highly-anticipated seven-volume series *Feeding Your Chakras* and co-authoring *Angelic Resonance* with international bestselling author Angela Orora Medway–Smith.

Sevante elevates humanity by nourishing the mind, body, and soul. Her passion is felt throughout all of her creations. She offers a deeper knowledge of Spirit and self-expansion to her community to have optimum emotional, mental, physical, and spiritual (EMPS) wellness.

She travels globally with Nourish Your Soul Retreats, speaks at holistic festivals worldwide, teaches online classes to become a certified intuitive food therapist, offers private readings and healing sessions online and in person, hosts the Nourish Your Soul show, and is expanding her Ayurvedic tea and incense imports from Nepal across the USA and Canada.

Sevante is nestled on a beautiful island in Southwest Florida with her husband, music producer Howard Merlin Wulkan, and their four-legged brood amongst palm trees, enchanted ponds, peacocks, and the best of Mother Nature's bounty.

Enter her world of nourishment and your next dimension of wellness at: https://linktr.ee/ciftofficial

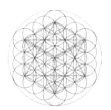

CHAPTER 3

SENSORY ALIGNMENT THERAPY

OVERCOMING LIMITS AND CLAIMING YOUR VALUE IN THE NOW

Dr. Heidi M. MacAlpine, OTD

MY STORY

"The present is the only time in which any duty can be done or any grace received."

~ C.S. Lewis

How do I take ownership of this part of myself that screams, 'Take control, girl'!?

Will this allow me to overcome my barriers and begin my journey without fear and self-judgment but with grace?

Indubitably!

I've come to believe grace can only be found when it's done in nonjudgmental baby steps, like learning to ski or ride a bike, which allows us to soften, be at ease, feel, and process information in a more gentle, kind, and meaningful way. By being in the moment with each step, one sense at a time, it gets easier to process the information and overcome barriers.

My practice and program, Sensory Alignment Therapy, was developed after experiencing different traumas that vibrated my core and shook the senses out of me until I was numb, weak, and lacked motivation. Dis-ease (Epstein Barr Virus, Lupus, Chronic Lymphocytic Leukemia, and Covid) took over my body with chaotic energy, wreaked havoc with my immune system, and knocked me flat on my back. A web of restrictions invaded my fascial system and body limiting my movement and ability to function at full capacity—a cruel joke fear played with me as it played hopscotch on my heart and hijacked my worth, value, and good moments (days at a time).

I learned that a greater awareness of myself (using the senses) was crucial, helping me to heal in small increments to enhance my quality of life.

Fear suspended me in time and space. The numbness and sadness created barriers to participating in the things I was passionate about, such as drawing, exercising, and socializing. My focus was on feeling better with less pain and inflammation. I no longer felt my zest and energy!

I distinctly remember the first time I decided to use two simple tools and techniques, a diffuser with lemon oil, which lifted my mood and made me a little more alert, and the myofascial techniques I'll share below with you, which decreased my inflammation and increased my movements.

If we were open to them, new opportunities for connection, meaning, and expansion were possible for me, and now my clients. Connection to our children brought me to my client, J., and I had the opportunity to share my tools and techniques with her.

J. was diagnosed with progressive multiple sclerosis (MS) in 2000. She was placed in a nursing home in 2019 due to her need for 24-hour care. I was excited to meet the mother of the bubbly young woman who brought joy to my son's heart and life (it might be more clear to say 'I was excited to meet my son's mother-in-law, the mom of the woman bringing joy to my son's heart.'), so I reached out via text to set up our first visit with one another in November 2022.

As I opened the door to her room, I stopped and absorbed the loveliness and comfort in small doses. J.'s room had character, humor, and sarcasm that instantly brought a connection and smile. As I entered her room, there was a black-and-white sign that said, "If at first you don't succeed, then maybe you just suck." Below the sign was an 11 x 15 colorful photo of her two children, aged four and seven, in a race car, like Thelma and Louise, the wind blowing their hair, and a zest for life on their faces. I flashed back to my children at that age. Next, my eyes shifted to the green-eyed tree frogs and Jesus wall stickers peeking behind, and next to different areas and objects on the wall. I laughed out loud at the monkey decals hanging from vines, holding photo frames with pictures of her children and family members. My attention was diverted to a saying to the right of her bed: "Prayer Changes Everything," with the prayers and a cross to the right of it. I paused for a moment longer and thought about her strong faith and spiritual belief. The more I spent with J. I became aware of how she claimed her space at the nursing home and devoted herself to prayer to stay grounded and create a safe and comfortable space. J. greeted me with a big smile, a soft hello, and kind brown eyes as I entered the room.

Has her kindness and faith always been a part of her? I admire that!

I know from my personal and professional experience that trauma or disability can change the way individuals move and think—shifts in our sense of safety and security alter our well-being, and put limitations on our movements and ability to want to engage in the things we need, love, and want to do.

J. begins our conversation via text with this statement: "It's taken me so damn long to figure out how to get here that I forgot what I wanted to say or write about. Thank you for your assistance Flash, and waiting for me to catch up mentally. Flash is the nickname she gave me because she says I'm filled with a lot of energy and involved in so much throughout the day. Now that I think of it, we're like the tortoise and the hare - remember that story? That's how I can feel frequently. The 'tiredness' that I felt was very much like what my MS felt like in the early stages, when I could walk. It felt like I had walked miles and miles. Just walking down the driveway to get the mail was equivalent to an expedition."

After reading her text, I asked her, "What would you like to gain from our time together and this experience?" The lack of sleep and energy made it difficult to have lengthy conversations. Through our conversations, I learned about the occupations that brought joy and meaning to J.'s life. Each visit and conversation helped me understand what made her tick.

We discussed her journey with MS since 2000, and the various therapies she explored to stay as functional and as pain-free as possible. She enjoyed teaching and being a mother to her two young adult daughters. She cherished the connections with her family and wanted to continue them and extend her kindness. She's an excellent listener with intelligence and a strong spiritual backbone!

I took the opportunity to have her collaborate with me on a couple of projects by considering her occupations and strengths (teacher, mother and friend, creativity, and strong writing skills). Her witty sense of humor became a part of our social engagements during visits. Being in the moment with J., I discovered that sleep deprivation diminished her ability to engage fully in the different things she loved and wanted to do. Engaging in meaningful conversation was challenging due to lack of sleep, low energy, and decreased attention and focus. This affected her desire to socialize for longer periods, and I respected her need to be alone and rest. I made it a point to make the most out of the activities and modalities we engaged in.

Aromatherapy is one of the simplest and most meaningful experiences with Sensory Alignment Therapy. This stimulated, entertained, and aligned her so that she could regulate her mood and energy in a natural, pleasurable, and non-threatening way. It was a beautiful thing to witness as the tailored and meaningful activity allowed her to become more interested, motivated, and engaged outside of the personal space she created.

Her thinking shifted and we created a tapestry of meaningful experiences that left us with a greater sense of well-being through our connection.

J. was given choices to decide the direction of our session by sharing research, information, and support that made her feel in control and safe. She chose to make a scrapbook and bridal shower collage for upcoming events in her daughter's life. We utilized our strengths and shared memories while choosing the photos for both projects. Her strongest and most frequently used sense, vision, and keen sense of detail, are what we relied on to collaborate and complete this project.

SHARPENING THE MIND AND OUR SENSES WITH PICTURES AND MEMORIES

As I enter the room, I smile as I feel the warmth of her space with the multitude of organized information on her walls that represents her. I'm once again visually stimulated by the flair and spice of her personality. Her personality and strengths shine through with the meaning of faith, family, and fun. Seeing and hearing how much her family meant to her we crafted a collage of our children at various ages for a bridal shower game. Each picture captured a story that strengthened our relationship and brought smiles to our faces and laughs that filled the room. We bonded and created meaningful moments to learn and grow through those memories, laughter, and smiles. I wanted to see more of those results.

BRINGING THE OUTSIDE IN

We continued to explore the use of different modalities to heighten her mood and improve her sense of well-being. As I enter her room, I hear a familiar greeting, "Hey, Flash!"

Although the room was filled with many pictures and objects, I didn't feel nature in her room. There were no plants, flowers, or greenery, like what I viewed from her third-floor window facing the courtyard filled with trees and flowers she couldn't see from her bed. After our previous conversation, I brought her a bouquet of her favorite flowers (daisies) and materials to make scented products (hand lotion and spray bottle), using the essential oils. The lavender hand cream and lemongrass aromatherapy lingered in her room and seemed to lift her mood, bring out her sense of humor, and make her smile. This expanded the energy in the room and brought out reciprocal conversations about memories of our children and the special times we shared with them. It also helped us complete our two projects for our children. It was lovely to share about our children, faith, and challenges. Through her sense of curiosity and openness to explore familiar and unfamiliar things, the outcome was greater than I anticipated and lasted throughout the week, until our next visit.

I sipped my morning coffee when I heard the ping of my cell phone. A text message appears from J: "There can be a lot of action going on and it seems like 'ping-ponging' back and forth in the room. Any chance I can get and remember to ask, I ask if they could spray the scent of lemongrass in my room. There was something about it. It made me happier."

She added, "Thank goodness you treated me before my daughter's wedding - it's great viewing all of the wedding photos! So, at bedtime, I felt happy, content, and relaxed. I slept well because I awoke at 5 a.m. instead of my usual 3-3:30 a.m. I felt differently too - I felt awake and refreshed!"

After our last session, she seemed to feel more at ease as the tension in her upper neck and back was released, using the four-inch myofascial therapy balls. She commented about feeling warmth in those areas and then started to turn her head from left to right as the corners of her mouth turned up and a satisfied look appeared.

I smile and bow my head.

Ping! Another message.

"Hey Flash! I'm feeling great today, thanks to you! I'm staring at the beautiful daisies and the lovely scented gifts. The flowers you arranged - it's amazing how something so simple can bring such happiness! Also, the wonderful lemon-scented oil massage to my hands has lasted into the next day leaving them warm and pink, instead of blue and feeling like ice! I'm looking forward to being with you again - you made my day! My week. Love, J."

This inspires and motivates me to continue to implement different modalities during my next visit. I noted the positive effects from vibration and frequency waves from music, singing bowls, and tuning forks. There's a shift in J.'s mood, energy levels, and sleep patterns. I chose to focus on different modalities that can be utilized with some research and support.

J. seemed agitated when I entered. Her eyes looked abnormally intense. She complained about not sleeping well, and meals and bathing being late due to a staff shortage that day. "My head is pounding!" she said.

HEIGHTENING THE SENSES OF TASTE AND SIGHT WITH GARDEN VEGETABLES

Incorporating fresh garden vegetables and stimulating different senses can create a more meaningful experience. I chatted with J. about the different garden vegetables we tasted growing up and the different senses they invoked, like their vibrant colors, earthy aroma, and the taste of a fresh red, plump, sweet tomato as we bit into it. Just as we finished, I mentioned my garden's growth stage at home. Just then her lunch arrived in cold metal containers, so she was unfamiliar with the meal. As I opened the container, she reacted, "Uuuhhg. Yuck!" There was a lack of color and vibrancy and the lettuce was limp and lifeless.

She wasn't fond of the bland nursing home food, the vibrancy and taste were nothing like the vegetables we grew up on. A light bulb went off!

Why can't I bring her vegetables from my garden for a fresh crunchy salad?

A big Cheshire Cat smile lit up her face and her light brown eyes turned earthy brown as she keenly eyed the freshly picked colorful salad. The freshness and taste of each veggie seemed to tantalize her taste buds and give her a new sense of arousal as she savored each bite. Her eyes widened and she was lost in the different flavors! One of the cherry tomatoes she ate was so juicy that it squirted out of her mouth and onto the blanket about a foot away from her! This simple gesture and experience brought the biggest change in her mood and energy.

Here are some comments from J. regarding the positive effects of the techniques and modalities used to improve her quality of life:

"The therapist being in 'tune' with my body and the utilization of various tools and activities such as myofascial release techniques and aromatherapy helped me to become more at ease with a decrease in muscle tension, contractures, and spasms."

"The results from the tuning forks are calming, particularly, when observing the actual physical vibrational movements, and hearing/feeling the tones emanating from them puts me in a more restful state and able to think more clearly. The brain fog isn't as significant."

Sensory Alignment Therapy has made some positive changes in not only my life but my clients' as well. It enables us to slow down, regulate, and align to the moment, and live life a little fuller. One sense. One moment. Each moment is lived with grace, trust, and ease.

Taking small actionable steps is key.

You can experience one aspect of this approach with these tools.

THE TOOL

SENSORY ALIGNMENT THERAPY USING THE THERAPY BALL

My experiences motivated me to develop my program, Sensory Alignment Therapy, to provide simple and effective tools to others. The method invites you to awaken, entertain, and align yourself with your eight senses (sight, sound, smell, touch, taste, proprioceptive, vestibular, and interoceptive). All these body systems (senses) allow us to perceive and process movement in an automatic and instinctual manner to gain a sense of safety and control to perform everyday activities. We treat the whole person (physical, emotional, spiritual, and social aspects), and gently remind ourselves of our value and uniqueness in the present space and time (the now!) in simple, achievable steps using our senses. This leads us to greater possibilities for healing. You may be overwhelmed with emotions, discomfort, and pain and wondering where to start. One of the tension-releasing exercises I mentioned earlier was the John F. Barnes Myofascial Release technique for the neck and shoulders using a small ball.

Let's take one step together today with the four-inch therapy ball. One that works best is an inflatable plastic ball or tennis ball, placed on the soft tissue (muscles) where the area of tension is felt.

Begin by placing the ball between you (area of tension) and the bed, chair, or wall, and gently lean into the ball with your body, moving it around until you find the tender or hard spot on the muscle. Then you can apply pressure and stay on the spot. Hold the pressure and allow the area to soften and release before moving the ball (three to five minutes minimum to receive the most complete therapeutic effect).

As a preventative measure, it's recommended that you consult with your healthcare provider before starting any new activities.

Enjoy a video to walk you through these steps here:

https://align-ot.ck.page/2de0f84540.

Dr. Heidi MacAlpine OTD, C-IAYT (500 hrs) CTP, has been a holistic occupational therapist for 35 years and is an expert devoted to working with people across the lifespan, including children and adults with special needs and their families. Her newly formed business, Align OT, has expanded her practice to working with health promotion and consulting in the community. Heidi's community-based practice tailors activities to meet the individual need(s) of her clients, using different platforms, such as the W.E.L.L. Matters Podcast, Meeting Your Needs radio show, and writing about the modalities in books.

Her extensive education and use of different modalities and tools throughout her career have enabled her to adapt and modify the tools and activities for a greater audience overcoming a variety of barriers. Her education, experience, and certifications such as JFB myofascial release techniques, trauma practitioner and trauma-informed yoga, Feldenkrais, and Stepping On Program have aided her in a newly developed program, Sensory Alignment Therapy. This program helps clients make subtle to big shifts in their minds and bodies while exploring new therapeutic tools and engaging in meaningful occupations. Through the exploration of different tools and modalities, the client gains a greater body awareness thorough individual choices that awaken, integrate, and align the nervous and sensory systems for a more meaningful and engaging experience.

Since graduating from Quinnipiac University (1989) and Boston University (2020) with a doctorate in Occupational Therapy, her mission is to improve the quality of life for herself and her clients through education, support, and the development of programs to improve the mental and physical needs of the community.

Heidi enjoys relaxing with a book and exploring sound and music, nature, dancing, and spending quality time with her husband, Ray, and their three children and granddaughter.

Connect with Heidi and find out more about Sensory Alignment Therapy:

Website: https://www.AlignOT.com

Podcast: https://www.buzzsprout.com/2293541

CHAPTER 4

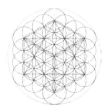

METACRYSTALS

EXPERIENCE THE MAGICK OF ARCHANGEL METATRON

Chrystal Rose, The Healing Medium

MY STORY

888. Eight! Eight! Eight! the magick number is perfect for 2024!

"Caw, caaaw, caaaawww!" came the sound from the tree branch above, interrupting my creative thought process.

"Hello, beautiful!" I said aloud to the bold crow as she met my gaze, "Thank you for your confirmation message!"

Princess Ciao Bella hopped beside me, her fluffy white dog ears flapping in the breeze. Despite having only three working limbs, the joyousness of being out on a sunny April day emanated from her in waves as we continued on our mindful walk.

A numerological 8, (2024 = 2 + 0 +2 + 4 = 8) yeeesss it makes sense for Archangel Metatron to use the infinity symbol in his healing, as he has before.

I best pop some bread out for the bird when we get home.

Hmm, stars have wonderful symbology as sigils.

My vivid imagination flitted from idea to idea as I tried them on for size.

The street was empty as an angel feather of white blew across my path.

Aaah, thank you, that's two signs in quick succession, I wonder if I'll get a third?

All things come in threes is a belief I've carried through lifetimes, a self-fulfilling prophecy perhaps.

On our illustrious arrival back to the castle (okay, it's just a humble abode, but 'an Englishman's home is his castle,' we say), I grabbed some flatbreads for the crow, and proceeded to scatter them on the grass on the opposite side from where I conversed with the blue-black bird.

"Swoosh!"

The crow alighted onto the bank where I scattered the bread and swiftly flew back up to the roof of a neighboring home to alert her mate.

"Swoosh!"

The pigeons toyed with the idea of joining them thinking better of it, and patiently waited from a distance as the crows had first dibs on the scraps.

And there it was, my third sign. I fed the birds occasionally, but the crow had been perched on the opposite side of the houses and somehow knew I'd bring her food to this location. Priceless! Spirit in play. No profiling is needed!

So here I am, writing my second collaborative chapter on healing. Well, it's not wise to upset a crow—there may be a murder.

As a child, I had a blackbird join me on any walks or cycle rides along the country lane through the hamlet of Snailwell on the outskirts of the racing town of Newmarket. I consider them to be one of my spirit animals and their presence brings me peace.

MetaCrystal Healing was born on Wednesday, the 17th of April 2019, as I tuned into the Aquamarine Dragon of Neptune from the Dragon Oracle by the wonderful Earth angel Diana Cooper. Incidentally, this was just over a month since I channeled Divine Energy Healing. The Universe was certainly keeping me busy.

This sacred dragon soul was to assist in my spiritual development, and I intended to update my crystal training. As we are ever-evolving in our learning, it's prudent to include current understanding as teaching and learning are inextricably linked. Education is something we never finish.

Candle lit, incense burning, phone off, feet up, let's see what she has to say.

Visions of sacred symbology played as a film within my mind's eye, including Metatron's cube and various other geometric shapes from within the flower of life. I found myself joined by the archangel Metatron (the 'voice of God'). It seems I have a penchant for working with the animal kingdom, and as I had with my angel oracle in the past, the frequency of classical music filled the air around me. Oddly, the only time I listen to this genre is upon writing up spiritual works.

Angels are believed to hail from Sirius and the Pleiades. From our human construct, we tend to think of life on other planets as only able to exist if water is present. If we consider that we are spirits having a human experience, not humans having a spiritual experience, and realize that we all house a divine spark as creations of God in his likeness, then accept that in our purest form, we are light or energy. The need for physical sustenance is then null and void. Intelligent life on other worlds within the universe, and indeed multiverse, becomes obvious, and the arrogance of thinking that we are 'it' falls away.

My meditative walk took place on April 8, 2024, before the meeting of the authors of this collaborative work, amid a recent solar eclipse, new supermoon, and mercury retrograde. I wondered if I chose the Chinese curse to live in interesting times, and it occurred to me that this affects the whole, not just the sum of the parts, so much healing would be needed especially at this time and as Laura Di Franco reminds us often, we aren't just ordinary, we are badass!

Our Zoom meeting kicked off with an unabridged version of a poem of encouragement she created that same morning, suggesting, among other pearls of wisdom, something along the lines of that we should embrace our 'witchy' selves. Perfect, considering my crow visitation earlier (as I prefer to think of them as ravens, as they're in the same family of avians). I'm also 'owned' by Bluebell, a beautiful black cat, so I fit the mold. Anyone with a feline can vouch for them maintaining their goddess personality and sense of entitlement from Egyptian times when they were revered.

Anyway, 'back to the knitting' as Angela, my good friend and lead author, will often say. My crystal teachings were about to take on a whole new life

Ooh, working with elemental grids of fire, earth, air, and water for the healing of Gaia fits so nicely with Divine Energy Healing!

Gosh, Spirit is certainly keeping me busy. I wonder why, but why now?

Well, nothing is ever truly coincidental, is it?

Considering the lessons within our first Energy Healer's Oracle chapter on Divine Energy Healing and elemental mindfulness, I'm reassured everything is exactly to plan and how it should be in Divine timing. Time is a human tool, of course, which quantum physicians have found not to be linear but more coexisting as past, present, and future in nature, but this is a whole subject in its own right.

Crystals, as a tool for healing that's accessible to all, are part of the Divine mission of illuminating the darkest corners of the Earth with this loving energy.

Level one, 'MetaCrystals,' includes a sacred geometric layout, as well as everything you need to know for the safe and efficient use of crystal therapy. Although my original course already included three levels, the updates given were to prove out of this world.

The archangels are to be front and center of your teachings from level two MetaCrystals. We will unravel the sacred wisdom of the flower of life together.

Fun! Fun! Fun! This doesn't feel like work at all!

Usually, I find studying of any sort a chore, but I found myself not only energized but enthused and excited about the grids and layouts given to me to pass on to others.

Over the coming days, with my pad and pen, I sat down to gain inspiration for improving level three. Inhaling deeply and exhaling fully, the blissful sensation of relaxation enveloped me in a cocoon as messages flooded in.

Listen in and listen well. We need your full attention for a little while. Fifteen archangels wish you to notate a message from them for others to include in your manual.

Are you kidding me, fifteen? I'm not sure I can concentrate for that long.

You can and you will. It'll be easy; you only need to listen.

Well, we know that's not my strong point, but hey ho, here I am, fire away.

Right on cue, the archangels introduced themselves and imparted their knowledge and sterling advice with sigils and particular crystals to pass on. Their discussion about love and positivity was inspiring, and I felt honored to be in their presence. It occurred to me that these highly evolved beings, whilst all working for the creator with various advice, all maintained unique personalities just as we do.

Archangel Ariel, with her predilection towards the environment, was to be the cornerstone, so to speak.

Whilst I in no way promote or condone doing anything other than focusing fully on your driving whilst in charge of a moving vehicle, the nuts and bolts of this chapter were recorded on the M25, the circular motorway around London, UK. I stopped at South Mimms service station to give Bella a leg-stretch and phone my youngest brother to alert him to my imminent arrival and for him to pop the kettle on. I also set the recorder to hands-free. As I recorded, whilst continuing to carefully steer in the driving rain, with the windscreen wipers squeaking away, it seemed my navigational skills had eluded me.

Oh, how have I reached the Dartford Tunnel without realizing it? I must've missed the M11. Oh, feck!

On some level, I knew that this was Spirit's intention, but later I questioned why I couldn't have continued with it on the M11 towards my birthplace of Newmarket, Suffolk. It is, I'm told, to do with the ley lines and energy of the capital city. Oddly, I've always felt most at home within an hour of the big smoke. City life is not for me as I love the countryside and consider myself more of a towny. My family home is now an hour south and my mother hails from Kent, the garden of England.

What follows is a transcript from Archangel Metatron given on the orbital motorway (whilst heading back towards the M11 turnoff):

Well, here I am, 'the voice of God' as you so eloquently speak! I wish to convey all of God's teachings on the healing of humanity and all life, the flora and fauna, as you say, the waterways, the landways, and the airways.

Once you reach a state of bliss, a vibrational ascendancy, you will realize that this will come naturally; there is no need to do anything different from what would come naturally. You would naturally look after the animals; you would naturally look after the beautiful Earth that you have been made guardian of. You have been gifted guardianship of the beautiful world, and this is something that has been forgotten.

Life is not hierarchical. You are here as part of the cycle of life. A circle of life– all life is interlinked. You are here to love and care for the animals and the birds and the trees and the flowers, not to cut them down and abuse your place. One could say you've 'looked a gift horse in the mouth.'

There is nothing I can tell you in truth that you don't already know. As an aspect of the Divine, you are aware of all of the wisdom and all of the power of the universe within you. My only request is that you awaken to this truth, and if you can do this, and another does this, and another does this, it will exponentially cause you to be your saviors.

You are creating the world in which your children will live and your children's children. It cannot continue the way it is. Start to make decisions within your spheres, in your little worlds, tending to your gardens and this will cause healing on a global scale.

I leave you with this message in love, light, and truth.

And so, it is.

Praise be to Yahweh!

Archangel Metatron is calling upon us to make an informed decision to become the best version of ourselves. This will have a positive effect on those around us and everyone we come into contact with. So herein lies the key to healing the world around us.

Here are my musings on practical things we can do, such as recycling:

- Making compost.
- Using water butts to water grass and flowers.
- Using reusable plastics.
- Repurposing glass jars.
- Upcycling old furniture.
- Buying pre-loved clothing.
- Donating unused clothes to charity.
- Planting a tree.

Fossil fuels aren't infinite and incorporate greener energy such as solar or wind turbines until we have more efficient ways. Whichever are the latest, cleanest methods to use are preferable. Our seas are no longer to be dumping grounds. Healing of the air, earth, water, and fire including the volcanic region of the Pacific Ring, and spirit.

Now, planting a tree is an interesting one. Whilst conducting a pilot of MetaCrystals with a friend, during the Earth grid layout I was shown two citrus trees, which I was to place on either side of the yard of my then spiritual center. A little while later, I purchased two of these with a spherical shape from a local garden center and did just that. It seemed that these were acting as guards aside the walk-through, not unlike those in the Glastonbury Chalice Wells entrance oak trees, but of course, a much scaled-down version in pots. On departing the center, a couple of years later, I found I couldn't save them in my garden, still in their pots, but the souls departed, leaving only dead trees. They fulfilled their purpose.

I'm sure you can think of many more helpful ways of healing our environment. Let's make it our mission.

A little about my mediumship:

- Sitting weekly in a meditation circle has paid dividends for my personal spiritual development.

- I'm a regular platform medium and provide services at spiritual churches.

- I never take this for granted, but having said that Spirit has never yet let me down. My team of guides (Super troopers) includes my Liverpudlian dad, family helpers, angels, and archangels.

- It's wonderful to be able to communicate via technology to people over the other side of the world in a three-way conversation with heaven. If you'd like me at your church or community center, please drop me a line.

- There is simply nothing better than the upliftment brought to self and others through mediumship.

A little about crystals:

- Crystals worn or placed around the home act as energy emitters, as they give off a piezoelectric charge and also dispel negativity. I could write a whole book on this alone, but if you're reading this it's likely that you use them already or are drawn to them without quite knowing why. If using them in this way, the larger rough stones are preferable as children can easily mistake tumblestones for candy.

- Cleanse them often by running them under a tap or using rainwater from your water butt. As a rule of thumb, refrain from cleansing anything ending in 'ite' with water as they may disintegrate, and instead use an alternative such as incense.

- Contraindications include having a pacemaker, the first trimester of pregnancy, and severe mental illness.
- Crystals you're drawn to are generally the ones most beneficial for you.

THE TOOL

Below is an efficient method of swiftly cleansing, clearing, and energizing your chakras, to be utilized on its own or before conducting crystal therapy.

1. Draw a large figure 8 on the floor in front of you with your mind's eye, with a pointy finger or crystal wand. Start from the middle and draw the first line to the left following it around and back to the center. The figure itself can be drawn either upright or sideways as an infinity loop, as is your preference. Cupping a crystal within the three remaining fingers, if you're pointing, will enable you to house this energy within the gem, and this can be your activating stone for using this tool in the future.

8

Repeat these two more times, atop the first 8, thrice in all.

2. Step onto the center point of the eight.

3. Now visualize the three eights you've drawn staying joined in the middle but separating as a six-petalled flower (Aphrodite's flower) and see them beginning to rotate as fan blades anti-clockwise.

4. They rise through your feet and turn sideways to face your spine from the front.

5. With each inhalation, the symbol spins upwards, cleansing and clearing each of the main chakra points in turn, including the upper heart or thymus.

Starting with the base, then the sacral (positioned below the naval), the solar plexus (positioned where the ribs join at the base), the heart (central chest), the upper heart (upper chest), the throat (base of the neck), the third eye (slightly above and between your physical eyes), your crown (the top of your forehead).

6. Up to the Soul Star chakra approximately half a meter above your physical form, where it slows, ceases momentarily, transmuting all detritus to the Divine light, and begins to spin clockwise.

7. The fan blades (petals) then descend through the chakras in turn. Crown, third eye, throat, upper heart, heart, solar plexus, sacral, base.

8. Then down to the Earth Star chakra, situated approximately half a meter below your physical body. The fan then ceases momentarily, releasing any detritus to Mother Earth, and then spins anti-clockwise to repeat this cycle two more times.

On completion, the triple 8 ceases to spin and rests within your Earth Star chakra for future use.

To call upon this tool again, the following incantation may be used, or not, along with holding your chosen crystal. Clear quartz, the master crystal, is suggested due to its versatile nature, although any you prefer will be perfect for you.

"Eight by the power of three

Spin up widdershins

Spin down deosil

Thrice my power back to me

And so it is, so mote it be."

This tool can be used daily, and if housed within your crystal, with practice it can be utilized quickly and efficiently.

Further to this, there is access to an Archangelic Metatron's Cube crystal layout from the Divine Energy International website in the links.

Chrystal Rose Addison is CEO of Divine Energy International Ltd, a nonprofit organization established in 2020 to promote energy healing. Notably, she is the originator of Divine Energy Healing, which she was blessed to have channeled directly from Source in 2019, and a co-author of the multinational bestseller, Volume I of *The Energy Healer's Oracle*.

Chrystal Rose is a Spiritual Medium and Master Teacher of Divine Energy Healing (naturally) - MetaCrystals – Angelic Medium - founder of the Pyramid Healing System - Shaman of the Munay Ki - Violet Flame and Lady of Silver - Pendragon Reiki - and Universal Life Church Minister.

Chrystal was a member of the Royal Navy Senior Service, traveling to many countries around the world, and later pursued a career in Primary Education.

She resides with her husband on the UK South Coast offering accredited training courses both online and in person.

Chrystal is happiest when she is with her adult boys or shouting encouragement from the stands when supporting them in playing for their respective teams in professional soccer matches.

Connect with Chrystal Rose:

https://linktr.ee/chrystalrose47

https://www.divineenergyinternational.com

https://Instagram.com/divine_energy_international

https://www.linkedin.com/in/divine-energy-international-0332a2246

https://youtube.com/@DEI1111

CHAPTER 5

HOLISTIC METAMORPHOSIS

WHAT TO DO WHEN NOTHING ELSE IS WORKING

Jennifer Palmer, Transformational Healer/Teacher

MY STORY

God, are you there? Help me. Please.

I lay in the chamber, sobbing in desperation, with my mind racing. My heart pumped with fear and ached for answers. All of my armor and resistance suddenly dissolved. I surrendered.

Tears streamed down my face as I prayed these words to the only presence in my life that I had any bit of faith in.

Nothing is working, and I can't continue like this. If you show me how to heal us, I promise you I will dedicate my life to helping others do the same. I need your help.

I was in a small hyperbaric oxygen chamber with my two young boys, passing the oxygen mask back and forth. Both of my boys wore headphones and watched movies on their devices. I can't tell you how grateful I was that my boys couldn't hear me as I was having a seemingly one-sided conversation with an invisible being who was supposed to save me. They probably would've thought I'd lost my mind.

It was hot, sweaty, cramped, and uncomfortable. I felt the increased pressure in my head and face as the pressure in the chamber helped to bring oxygen more deeply into our bodies. It was a small chamber for even one person, but all three of us were crammed into this tiny space. I desperately sucked in oxygen through the shared mask, hoping to heal, and prayed life would get better.

Did I mention I was desperate?

I suffered from chemical sensitivity, chronic pain, and muscle weakness. Certain specific toxic exposures exhausted me. Sometimes, it was too painful to walk. I had an overburdened immune system, hypothyroidism, and chronic digestive issues, and my body was just barely coping. My oldest son, Jacob, was on the autism spectrum, and my youngest son, Nathan, had asthma and eczema. We were all suffering, and I felt like a terrible mom as I watched our family struggle.

So yeah, I was beautifully desperate. So much so that I surrendered everything I thought I knew so that I could receive what I needed.

My mind continued racing, and my heart continued opening.

Is this my life?

What am I doing wrong?

I'm so scared that we will never heal.

Please, God. Please help us.

How did this happen?

What can I do?

How can I help my boys?

What is the purpose of all of this illness and suffering?

Are you there? Do you hear me? Am I worthy?

I didn't receive an answer at that moment, but I did feel better for having surrendered my fears and frustrations to a higher power. What I didn't know at the time was that these questions created an opportunity for God (Creator/Universe) to respond soon after that. That was the moment that changed everything and activated my purpose to help others with their healing journey. It was a moment I'll never forget and will always be grateful for.

About a week after that moment in the chamber, I met with a doctor who was clearly part of God's response to my plea for help. He said, "You have had a lot of trauma in your life, and this is keeping you from getting better." He sent me to a counselor who practiced different alternative modalities that could help with trauma, and it opened up a new world of understanding for me.

What I learned from seeing that enlightened counselor:

- You can heal trauma and emotions to improve your health and your life.
- Your thoughts and beliefs affect your outcome.
- There is always purpose in our challenges.
- You can forgive even the most difficult things.
- Forgiveness heals.

Around the same time, I started to learn about energy healing, and I took my first Reiki class.

Whoa - I can feel the energy coming out of my hands. This is real!

Am I doing this right?

I just saw a vision. I'm a freaking intuitive!

There is so much I do not understand. I'm just a computer programmer, after all. What the heck am I doing?

Now I need to really dive in. I have a lot to learn.

This is a sacred calling. It's what I asked for. It's what I promised. This changes everything.

Lookout, world, here I come!

And there I was. I was going down the Reiki rabbit hole, and I knew it was exactly what I was supposed to do as part of my promise to God. As I was taking classes and practicing my newfound skills, I also healed myself.

I healed deeply.

As I offered energy healing to more people, I was challenged with new and different concerns. I realized there was more I needed to understand about healing. I saw that some people healed more easily than others. I had some clients whose lives completely changed for the better in one session, but I had other clients whose issues never seemed to budge.

How do I help my clients who aren't healing?

I connected with my spirit guides one day so I could better understand how to help my most challenging clients. I started to get information about the mindset and awareness of those who heal. I started to see patterns in my clients and in me, that kept us stuck.

Many words of wisdom came through that day. The most profound for me was that there is no true power outside of the vibration of divine, unconditional love.

You cannot be in the vibration of love when you feel fear, shame, guilt, anger, hatred, sadness, resentment, apathy, or any other lower vibrational emotion. If there is any separation or resistance, you're not in the divine love vibration. It's a choice to be in one or the other.

I had many thoughts about this.

Okay, but how do we move through that lower vibrational emotion to get into divine love?

I mean, sometimes people have a righteous reason to feel these things. We surely cannot be love and light all the time, can we?

Dude–sometimes it feels good to be mad.

And what is divine love exactly?

My guides answered, and I learned a lot. What they taught me is that true divine love is a state of acceptance of all that is. It's moving beyond the need for forgiveness and out of the triggered state that caused us to close our hearts and our minds. It's the highest state of respect, appreciation, and gratitude, knowing that none of us are perfect and some people may purposefully choose to cause harm to another.

In this state, we take self-love to a whole new level by knowing how to advocate for what we want or need in any situation or relationship. We do not allow someone else to cause harm to us, and we do this lovingly, respectfully, and even with gratitude.

Sometimes, that's way easier said than done. I work at this every day, and I'm not perfect. I often find myself out of that state of divine love, but usually briefly, as I realign to the higher vibration. It's always when I feel victimized by what someone has said or done. I know that if I respond to someone or something when I'm not in a divine love state, it doesn't go well. If I can align to divine love, I'll have a much easier experience and a better understanding of what's going on with the person, me, or the situation.

Divine love is not about being a doormat. It's not about excusing the actions of others. It's not about blame or shame in any way. And you certainly can't be in divine love when you're seeing yourself as a victim. Any time you see yourself as a victim, you're powerless and in a lower vibrational state.

Divine love is about processing what happens in this experience from a wise space and not processing it from the trigger. The trigger is where we're closed off from love, and it's incredibly difficult to heal in that space. Put the trigger on the shelf temporarily and get into divine love. That's where the magic occurs and you can more accurately see the situation to know what to heal or how to respond.

After spending some time integrating what I learned from my guides about the consciousness needed to heal, angels began showing up during healing sessions. They called themselves the Oroshom and described their purpose as helping with the ascension process by healing traumas and raising our vibration. They explained that the process of healing is an upward spiral where energy meets consciousness and that we must raise our consciousness and bring in specific energy frequencies to heal deeply at the same time.

I have spent a lot of time with these energies, healing myself. It cleared baggage, ancestral patterns, and karma. It healed deep and old trauma. Because of this work, my health and the health of my boys greatly improved.

When I started utilizing the Oroshom Angel energy in my client sessions, along with the consciousness and wisdom from my guides, my challenging clients started to shift. We were clearing entities and parasitic energies, past life trauma, karma, family patterns, belief blocks, and so much more.

I started taking notes after sessions because the angels were showing me techniques and ways to harness the energy to get the desired outcome. I began to realize I was meant to teach this information and techniques to others. As I started teaching, my students experienced dramatic transformations in their lives. As they practiced on others, their clients started having dramatic shifts as well.

What a blessing it is to see lives change for the better. It's not always an easy path, but you can heal, and you can heal very deeply. Your life can be completely transformed. Imagine what your life could be like if your heavy baggage and traumas were resolved.

Are you ready to heal and transform your life?

THE TOOL

Holistic Metamorphosis (HM) is a unique modality and a result of spending many hours with the Oroshom angels and my spirit guides. It's meant to help us understand this ascension process we're in as souls and to help us heal what's holding us back.

There are many things that HM energy can help to clear and heal:

- Personal and ancestral karma
- Negative beings, influences, and energies
- Trauma throughout your soul's history
- Lower vibrational emotions
- Vows and contracts
- Ancestral patterns
- Beliefs and resistance

Why is this important? These things that we clear are literally weighing down your vibration. Raising our vibration is vitally important for our ascension and our life's journey. Just about every client I work with says they feel so much lighter after our sessions. That's because they are!

Does it permanently clear these issues? Yes. However, new challenges may arise for you. Life seems to be a series of lessons and tests followed by healing and growth. HM is a tool to help you for the rest of your life.

One of the best things you can do frequently is cleanse your chakras. This helps to clear out some of these heavier energies and it helps to raise your vibration.

You can do this as a general cleansing or with a specific intention. I highly recommend having a specific intention. For example, you may want to focus the cleansing on the loss of a relationship or maybe a specific health concern. You can tell the energy to help you specifically with that issue, and then you can also ask it to help you with whatever else needs to be cleansed for your highest good.

You may want to journal what you notice at each chakra as sometimes you may become aware of old wounds. You may also have sudden inspiration or awareness of something. It's okay to write things down during the process as sometimes you may forget if you wait until the end.

CREATE SACRED SPACE

Creating a clear and sacred space is an important part of any spiritual practice. You want to make sure you are creating the best environment for your specific purpose with the practice. There are many types of beings and energies out there, and you'll want the clearest space possible whenever you spiritually connect, receive intuitive information, or work on healing.

1. Hold out your hands in front of you and imagine a ball of pure and powerful white light energy in your hands. Try to feel the energy and connect with it. Tell that ball of energy that it's to clear you and your space of all energies and beings not of divine love or not here to help you with healing.

2. See that ball of white light energy get bigger until it fills the room you're in or the immediate ten feet of space around you.

3. Call in the Oroshom angels or Archangel Michael to hold this as a sacred space for your healing.

4. Close your eyes and get comfortable. Take a moment to feel what it's like to be in your body and be as joyful as possible in the moment. If you're feeling really low, you can still do this. But, do your best to at least be in faith and trust in God. Try not to dwell on the issues that are upsetting you.

CHAKRA CLEANSE

1. Envision another ball of pure white light and state your specific intention for healing and clearing if you have one.

2. Imagine that ball of white light coming up through your feet, slowly working its way up your legs to your root chakra at the base of your spine. At the root chakra, it pauses and starts spinning. It pulls out all the heavy energies that you no longer need. See it there until the root feels cleared or for about a minute.

3. As the ball keeps spinning, it slowly moves up the main channel of your spine to the sacral chakra just below your belly button and pauses there. It pulls out all the heavy energies that you no longer need. See it there until the sacral feels cleared or for about a minute.

4. The ball slowly moves up the main channel of your spine to the solar plexus chakra just above your belly button and pauses there. It pulls out all the heavy energies that you no longer need. See it there until the solar plexus feels cleared or for about a minute.

5. The ball slowly moves up the main channel of your spine to the heart chakra in the center of your chest and pauses there. It pulls out all the heavy energies that you no longer need. See it there until the heart feels cleared or for about a minute.

6. The ball slowly moves up the main channel of your spine to the throat chakra in the center of your throat area and pauses there. It pulls out all the heavy energies that you no longer need. See it there until the throat feels cleared or for about a minute.

7. The ball slowly moves up the main channel of your spine and through your head to the brow chakra at the forehead and pauses there. It pulls out all the heavy energies that you no longer need. See it there until the brow feels cleared or for about a minute.

8. The ball slowly moves up the main channel to the crown chakra at the top of your head and pauses there. It pulls out all the heavy energies that you no longer need. See it there until the crown feels cleared or for about a minute.

9. See the ball shoot out of your crown and out to the universe. Give gratitude for the cleansing, knowing that you have cleared all that can be cleared for now. Feel connected to your body and slowly open your eyes.

10. Notice what you feel in your body. Notice what you think and feel about the situation you intended cleansing for. Do you have any new awareness?

CHAKRA TRANSMUTATION FLAME EXERCISE

If you want to take chakra cleansing to the next level, go to the link below and receive a powerful chakra transmutation flame chart and cleansing exercise. It's part of my Holistic Metamorphosis Foundation class and I think you will enjoy it.

https://www.jenn-palmer.com/getchart

Jennifer Palmer is a transformational healer, intuitive, teacher, and spiritual coach. She is the founder of a large wellness center in Maryland where she fell in love with her clients and students, honed her skills, and practiced her healing work for 13 years. She is the Creator of Holistic Metamorphosis, an energy-healing modality that helps with each person's ascension process.

Jennifer also has a doctorate in Traditional Naturopathy and is a Master teacher of Usui Reiki and Karuna Reiki. She has studied many energy healing techniques, such as mediumship, Life Force Healing, Access Consciousness, and Arcturian Healing Light. She specializes in clearing entities and healing the energy connected to trauma and difficult experiences.

Jennifer believes in a mind-body-spirit approach to healing; that the whole person needs to be nourished with love, joy, and good food, and detoxified from spiritual, mental, emotional, and physical toxins. She works from the premise that we need to clear out what isn't serving, and bring in what does and that our minds need to be positively cultivated and healed of negative thought patterns and traumas.

She has developed a series of courses called Healing Activation Program (HAP) that is designed to help delve into the healing journey, either as a client or a rising energy healer in training. She believes energy healing is a beautiful and sacred gift to humanity that is meant to be shared.

Her favorite phrase is, "The bigger the catalyst, the further you can catapult." Her passion is to help people use their challenging situations to their advantage so they can advance as souls and achieve as much as possible in this lifetime in alignment with their soul's mission.

Connect with Jennifer today, sign up for her newsletter, and change your life!

Website: https://www.jenn-palmer.com

Newsletter: https://www.jenn-palmer.com/newsletter

Holistic Metamorphosis:
https://www.jenn-palmer.com/holistic-metamorphosis
Healing Activation Program:
https://www.jenn-palmer.com/HealingActivationProgram
Facebook: https://www.facebook.com/jenniferruhlpalmer
Facebook Group:
https://www.facebook.com/groups/ascensionactivationhealing
Instagram: https://www.instagram.com/jennpalmerhealer
YouTube: https://www.youtube.com/@JennPalmerHealer

CHAPTER 6

AKASHIC RECORDS

THE LIBRARY OF LIVES:
HOW TO RELEASE SELF-DOUBT FOR GOOD

DebS, Energy Release and Akashic Records Facilitator

MY STORY

"When did you last go to the library to get a book then?"

"Probably not since I was a kid I would think. No, wait; I do remember going to our local community library a few years ago, but their selection wasn't great, and they didn't stock the books I wanted. I could've ordered them, but it would have taken a few weeks, and I just couldn't wait, so I ended up buying them myself!"

I couldn't see through the windows of the small café my friend and I sat in as they were steamed up due to the typical cold, wet Welsh weather. The gorgeous bitter aroma of coffee and the damp warmth wrapped themselves around us like a big warm Welsh 'cwtch' (hug).

We chatted about therapy books we were reading, energy therapies and how phenomenal they are, and how—even with all the variety of therapeutic modalities I learned over the past 30 years, together with numerous other workshops I attended—I still didn't have my therapy business up and running fully. I simply couldn't get to the bottom of why. I attempted it years ago and didn't like the inconsistency of income. Since then, I've always fitted it in around other steady jobs I've been fortunate to have.

"I just feel like I'll never get to find out. Why does it feel like it's hidden away from me like some weird secret I'm not party to? I don't understand how that one thing always evades me. It's so frustrating and annoying! Sometimes I feel that maybe I'm just not meant to be in this business."

"Well, I believe you are, and I can understand how frustrating that might be for you. I also think I may have something that could help."

"Really? I think I've tried pretty much everything that's out there, to be honest, and still no joy. You know how many different courses I've done over the years, all of which I loved, but still didn't get the business going properly?"

"I know, but each one has added to your skill set, and you got what you needed from them on a personal level, didn't you? Anyway, what if I were to tell you there's a library that contains all the information about every single life you've ever lived, and you can get access to it yourself? Think about it; it might contain the answers you've been looking for!"

Every life? All in one place? What on Earth is she on about? Has she finally lost her marbles?

For some reason, my skeptical mind leapt straight to the fore which was so odd as I'm usually very open-minded.

"What on Earth are you talking about?"

"I've heard recently about something called the Akashic Records, which is like an energetic library that contains every single bit of information about you. My current understanding is that it contains all your life's experiences, your traumas, your highlights, your memories—everything. It contains all the answers, and the best thing is that you can learn to access them yourself, and you can access other people's, with their permission of course. How exciting does that sound?"

Wow! Just imagine being able to go into a library and having access to all the information about yourself; that's truly mind-blowing if it's possible!

I forgot the whole conversation until about six months later when an opportunity to attend an Akashic Records course presented itself. When I saw the information, I felt that familiar feeling of excitement rising in my stomach and an intuitive knowing in my head. Just to make sure I made the right choice, I performed some energy kinesiology to validate my decision and got a huge 'yes', so I booked my place.

I instantly remembered the conversation with my friend but soon discovered the description she gave me back then didn't do the Records justice at all. There was so much to learn about the phenomenal knowledge, divine guidance, and access to the truth held in the Records. I also had no idea how sacred a process it was and what a privilege it would be to enter other people's Records and help them with their 'stuckness.'

As the course progressed through to advanced levels, though, I felt my confidence waning. Self-doubt and imposter syndrome kicked in. I was comfortable in my own Akashic Records, but. . .

Who the hell am I to be able to have such powerful access to the truth of everything for other people? How can I put myself out there as a channel for this and charge for it, too? I'm just me. I don't believe I possess any special skills or intuitive know-how. I wasn't aware of having been a spiritual being when I was a child, like some of my friends in this field. What on Earth am I doing, thinking that I can do this?

Like a frightened snail, I withdrew into my shell of self-doubt. I was reluctant to team up with the other course attendees to practice, and the barriers and blocks built up. My whole energy went into massive resistance, and I became stuck.

After a while of doing nothing with the Records, either my own or others, I knew if I didn't get my case studies finished, I wouldn't get my qualification. I wouldn't be able to add it to my insurance, never be able to use this phenomenal modality as part of my SuperSonicSelf business, and all the money I spent on the course would have gone down the drain. I couldn't afford to be this much of a failure either personally, or financially!

One night, I made a special effort to access my Records. I put the heater on in my gorgeous, peaceful shed space I created to either read in the summer, meditate, or just sit quietly. I plumped up the beautiful pink, turquoise, and green cushions, lit an incense stick, turned the main light off, switched on the beautiful, twinkly heart-shaped fairy lights, and sank back into the plush cushions on the ottoman covered in a gorgeous, soft, warm, fluffy cream throw. I closed my eyes and entered my Records.

Why do I feel like I can't do this? What is wrong with me? Where has all this self-doubt, lack of confidence, and imposter syndrome come from?

All I heard was silence. Nothing. Nada. Zilch.

I breathed deeply: gently in through the nose, holding it, and out slowly with the exhale (longer than the in-breath) to relax and de-stress my body.

I became still and listened again. I asked more questions.

Where have you gone? Why aren't you speaking to me? Why can't I hear you?

With each question, I felt desperation grow. I felt anxiety rise in my body. My body temperature increased, I started to sweat, and despite the deep breathing, my breaths became shallower.

I released the fear using one of the many self-help techniques I learned over the years.

I started with an energy release statement: "I give myself permission to release these blocks affecting my confidence and making me doubt myself; I release them from all levels and across all planes, times, levels of consciousness, and beyond."

I let the words flow from my mind, heart, and mouth as I also tapped on certain acupressure points because I knew how effective and soothing the gentle tapping on my body felt.

Why have I got these blocks? Why am I so afraid of failing? What makes me feel like such an imposter? Why is it the Akashic Records training that has brought this out? Where has this doubt come from? Why am I questioning myself and my abilities?

This last statement triggered tears, followed by deep wracking sobs that rose from my heart. I allowed myself to cry, to sob but kept tapping and releasing in between wiping my nose and eyes.

When I was empty, I fell back into the cushions. I felt exhausted. I hadn't experienced a release like that in years. My breathing started to regulate and become deeper; my eyelids felt heavy, my body relaxed and I almost fell asleep.

And then I heard a voice.

I think you needed that.

I forgot my Records were still open. I didn't have enough energy to ask those questions again, but I didn't need to, as my record keepers clearly had something to say anyway.

By means of that release, you cleared many of those blocks yourself. Congratulations. You do not realize how powerful and skilled you are. You have been programmed during many lifetimes to be humble, and opting for self-doubt at the slightest opportunity has become a pattern and habit, none of which serve your highest good. Would you like us to send healing to all these issues surrounding imposter syndrome and doubting your power and abilities?

"Yes, please."

Do you wish to know anything else before we clear all this?

I was too exhausted and wasn't that interested. I just wanted it gone, for good.

Allow yourself to drift and let the healing flow through you, your present life, and through all the lifetimes you have previously lived.

I lay there and felt more relaxed than in a long while. My energy became lighter as the healing continued, and I fell asleep.

When I woke, I knew something had shifted. I felt alive, full of energy, lighter, more optimistic, and ready to tackle my case studies.

During a break from preparing for my case studies, I watched geese taking flight over the estuary one sunny spring morning through the large scenic windows of a local restaurant. The sky was the most stunning cerulean blue with fluffy white cotton ball clouds scudding by. There were very few people around, so it was beautifully quiet. I felt at peace with the world, my hands warming around a cup of tea as I waited for my friend for our (once-in-a-while-much-needed) catch-up.

She arrived in a beautiful spiritual purple dress, her dark hair sleek and shiny and, as usual, a glorious smile across her face. We hugged (heart to heart, of course) and ordered her drink. During our conversation, I mentioned the Akashic Records and that I was about to finally start my case studies. She immediately offered to be one.

Mmm, that's intriguing. Why would she need to do that?

I knew that she had a generous heart, but I was surprised she felt she could gain any information that she couldn't glean from her usual channels. She's probably one of the most intuitive and spiritual people I know and has worked in an incredibly high level of spiritual energy for a long, long time.

"I'd like to feel the experience, as I've only ever once received an Akashic Records reading, and that was a long time ago, so it would be wonderful to experience it again cariad, and if it helps you get your case studies done, that would be even more perfect."

And so, we booked the date and time. I sent her the pre-session documents and put the date in my diary.

But as the date came nearer, nerves appeared.

Oh my goodness, why does someone of Angela's status and spiritual awareness want to be a case study for me with the Akashic Records? I presumed that she could access all the relevant information that she needed with her skills and abilities. She works with some of the highest spiritual realms, so I'm not sure what I can do to help her.

Self-doubt raised its ugly head again, but this was a different scenario than before; it held a different energy.

Well, there is always a reason for issues that come up, so I'd better check in with my Records to find out what's going on this time because I need to clear these before I do her session to afford it the respect it deserves.

I settled into my Records and was informed that this was a different situation—the self-doubt related to not being good enough, not being in the same league, as well as being afraid of not matching up to the expectations of someone I admire and someone whose opinion matters to me. It also involved being afraid of being seen as someone of a 'lesser' hierarchy and it went back to previous lives. I checked whether I needed to know more and was given a 'no', so I went through the gentle process of clearing and healing in my Records.

The day arrived that I was due to read Angela's records. I went through my usual routine of cleansing my room, using an aromatherapy spray to support the process, and opening my heart and my Records to enable myself to be a clear channel of pure love, light, and truth for my client.

The session was beautiful, funny, and informative, validated some information Angela already knew, and healed a splinter that had lodged in her heart—released vows, past-life interference, implants, genetic, religious, and archetypal imprinting, and more.

Why on Earth am I doubting, worrying, and getting anxious about this?

Because you care, a voice said. *Because you want to be the best facilitator you can be to help the people who come to you.* My record keepers supported me as I supported Angela. *Because you're human, with an ego and past experiences that needed to be cleared too, to enable you to be a clearer channel, to continue to move you towards your SuperSonicSelf.*

After that session, I wrote this poem, which describes how I feel about the privilege of being able to facilitate people in this sacred journey.

AMAZING AKASHIC RECORDS

The Akashic Record keepers
Are omnipresent, helpful, and wise
Because they hold all our information
That persists after our body dies.

I love this new GOD-like connection
That fills me up with knowing
To have a heart-felt chat
With all our energies flowing.

To help both myself and others too
The opportunities are endless
Releasing all that holds us back
From being 'SuperSonic'; this I bless.

Whilst entering into these records
The records of my soul
I realize that love, light, and truth
Have always made me whole.

I got my own validation from Angela Orora Medway-Smith's review:

"I am a spiritual channel, a teacher of many different healing modalities and intuitive development with over 35 years of experience working with the spirit world. I recently had an Akashic Records consultation with DebS. The whole process was incredible! Wonderful. From the thorough information sent beforehand, which helped me consider my questions for the reading, the professional reading process, and the exceptional healing of ancestral and genetic imprints that took place. I was able to tune in fully to the process, so I actually saw and felt what was happening. I would HIGHLY recommend an Akashic Records consultation with DebS."

High praise indeed.

I guess I am meant to be in this business after all!

THE TOOL

The chapter shows a couple of examples of how Akashic Records can be used to receive clarification, healing, and release from the Record keepers. I also released some of the issues myself using energy kinesiology together with my own version of an energetic release statement.

As I am a huge believer in teaching people to fish rather than simply serving them a fish on a plate, I decided to share another release technique I use frequently. You can use this for anything, but especially if you are experiencing discomfort, disease, anxiety, or stress and feeling this in your body.

Get yourself into a comfortable position and allow your breathing to regulate at its own pace. Imagine silver threads of light coming out of the crown of your head, from your heart, and your hara (just below your belly button). As they connect, send them up into the universe as you set your intention to receive only pure love, light, and truth.

Send golden threads of light from the base of your spine and the base of each of your feet which unite as they travel down through each layer of the Earth and allow them to wrap themselves around the core of Mother Earth to keep you grounded.

Place your hands over your heart and allow your breath to flow gently in through your nostrils (if that is comfortable for you to do). Breathe in for the count of four, hold for the count of six, and breathe out through your mouth for the count of eight, like a gentle sigh. Do this three times to relax you.

Then, with your next in-breath, say either to yourself or out loud (if you feel confident enough to do so), 'I breathe in love, grace, and forgiveness.'

Send your breath to the tight, tense, sore, or stressed part while expanding that area of your body, thus stretching it out. Hold for the count of four and then as you breathe out, say the words, 'I release all that is harmful to my health, detrimental and counter-productive to my well-being and my Highest Good.'

When you let your breath flow out, allow it to empty completely and then tighten your abdomen to push out any remaining breath, (if it's comfortable to do so) before breathing in again. Do this several times until you feel you're done.

Note:

- you may experience some physical releases such as yawning, sighing, or crying, or you may just feel that the discomfort has left you.
- if you struggle to imagine, then use whichever sense(s) you prefer, and please don't force this; it's all about allowing and being gentle with yourself.

DebS derives great pleasure from sharing her knowledge and self-help techniques that she has collected over the past 30 years, especially in assisting others in releasing their blocked energy. In her personal life, she pursues activities that bring her joy, such as singing, dancing, walking outdoors, taking photographs, playing rounders, going to the gym, and cycling.

DebS has also self-published her memoir, *The Day I Didn't Kill Myself*, as evidence to others that there is life after divorce, depression, and suicidal thoughts. Part of her healing journey began with learning various massage techniques. She was first introduced to Reiki by her counselor, and over the years, she has learned many modalities, including energy kinesiology, hypnotherapy, meditation facilitation, EFT, Helix Method®, therapeutic writing, Akashic Records, and Breakthrough Breathwork. Every intervention she has learned has contributed to her Realization, Release, Rescue, & Recovery stages, as mentioned in her chapter *Out of a Black Hole into the Light* in the book *100 Poems & Possibilities for Healing*. Writing words of gratitude and appreciation are all part of the Rejoice stage of healing.

To thrive, DebS continues to release any blocks and maintain her flow. She believes that having been through a healing process herself has been invaluable in enabling her to assist others through theirs. In her facilitation sessions, she employs various techniques she uses herself to release negative or stuck energy. She supports you in moving from stagnation to flow and empowers you to discover your true potential and find your SuperSonicSelf, whatever that means to you.

Her philosophy when working with others is, "I rise, you rise; we rise together."

To contact DebS, please email: hello@supersonicself.com

She would love to gift you a free audio of "The Tool" which you can receive by visiting https://www.supersonicself.com

CHAPTER 7

ALCHEMICAL CRYSTAL SOUND

HEALING THE HEART AFTER LOSS OR BETRAYAL

Angeline Poon, Quantum Alchemy Crystal Bowl Practitioner

MY STORY

"Are you all right? I think you need help, Angeline," said my friend Sean as I looked out of the window from his apartment and thought of jumping.

I do need help. I have been screaming inside for help for a long time, but I do not know how to ask for it. Maybe it will be easier if I jump? No! That will be the easy way out, and I will not let him get the better of me.

'Him' being my business partner, Kon. Five years in business together, and we were still losing money. He demanded I pump more money into the company and I had none left.

Kon always demanded more from the inception of the business—the best machines that suited his ideas, the talent that matched his high standards. The only thing he didn't do was make money.

"Everything has to be perfect before we can do business."

When will it ever be ready? It's been five years, and we're still not ready.

I cried out for my protector to save me. "Archangel Michael, I'm sorry I wasted the chance the last time I wanted out of the business. Please give me another chance, and I'll grab it with both hands, I promise."

A few months went by. I continued to meet up with Sean a couple more times to talk about what I was going through. Soon, it was time to renew Kon's employment pass, as he was a foreigner in Singapore, where our business was based.

No surprise when his renewal was rejected. He demanded I appeal against the rejection. I did, hoping secretly that it would be rejected again.

And then I received a call.

"Madam, we're calling regarding the appeal you have submitted. Unfortunately, we will not be giving him any working pass. He will have to leave the country once his permit expires."

Thank you, Archangel Michael, thank you so much. I will not waste this chance you have given me.

TWO YEARS LATER

"Mum, there's blood on the floor and the armchair," I called out after coming back from the market with Mum to check on Dad.

"There's more blood in the toilet, too," she cried back to me.

I looked at Dad, who was lying on the bed, looking very pale and weak. "I am calling 995, and you are going to the hospital now."

Hours later, he was discharged. "Your dad lost quite a bit of blood, but he is doing better now. We did an X-ray and found that he had a big tumor in his stomach. He has to see a specialist, and we have arranged one for him in two days."

"From the test and scans, he has stage-three stomach cancer, and we have to operate as soon as it can be arranged. Don't worry; after the operation and chemotherapy, he will be all right," the senior specialist assured us.

All went well, except for a few complications, as the specialist predicted. Then, one day, Dad couldn't get out of bed. We rushed him to the hospital. I visited him every day. He appeared to be getting better until one day, I simply couldn't wake him to take his medication. The nurses tried and failed. He just didn't wake up. They sent him to the ICU.

Two weeks later, he passed on.

During his funeral, I was mostly in a daze. I lost my voice two days later. There was so much pain in me, but I couldn't cry. I haven't cried since the night he passed.

Six months after he passed, I still went about in a daze, angry and frustrated. There was so much paperwork to be done, and I was exhausted. I was so tired I felt I could sleep for a month. But I couldn't sleep well.

"Why not try out a sound bath? They do offer group sound baths here," suggested my masseur, Brenda.

"What is a sound bath, and what can it do for me?"

"It may help you to understand more about yourself."

I decided to take a leap of faith and gave it a go.

Wow, my first session of the sound bath was amazing. The mixture of singing bowls and gongs soothed my pains and swept them away. I hadn't felt so calm and light for a long time. I knew my body was asleep earlier, but I felt like I was in between being asleep and being awake, like I was floating. There were so many colorful lights, like watching a light show—so beautiful. What I remembered most was a seed growing into a seedling and into a beautiful tree. The message that came with this vision—*Be like the tree, standing firm no matter what*—hit me.

"Jane, I'm so into sound baths now, it helps with that dull ache I have around my heart area. I didn't know it was there until the ache lessened," I told my friend over coffee one day.

"Why not go learn how to play? We can go together. Let's go choose a bowl and start our lesson."

We made the appointment to see the trainer, Serena, to choose our own alchemy crystal singing bowls before we could start the lesson.

As she had many bowls on display, we were told to choose one that called to us. Not expecting what elements to choose, I found the one that called out to me the most—an F-note, Larimar bowl.

"You have to work on your heart, is that right? This bowl called out to you, telling you she can help you with heart healing," said Serena.

She was right. When I played the bowl, her singing went straight to my heart, so gentle and warm. It felt like I was being embraced in a very loving hug. It felt like love, and a realization came:

I finally know what unconditional love is. This is what I want to do; I want to share this feeling of unconditional love and share this method of healing through the sound of the alchemy crystal singing bowls.

I played them mainly for myself for years, healing my exhausted body, mind, and soul. They helped me to connect and understand my body. I began to understand the resentment, anger, fear, and anxiety all trapped in my stomach area and how they affected my health and size. Friends around me started to see the changes in me and how my looks changed.

"You look like you ate a light bulb," said a friend, describing a light in me she hadn't seen before. After months of staying at home due to COVID-19, I finally sat down to have lunch with my two besties. "How did that happen? Can you play for us too?"

Playing for friends started as a way for me to practice, and at the same time, firmed my resolution to make this part of my service to others. Seeing how they smiled so gently and calmly when they first opened their eyes after a session brought me so much joy. Knowing I could help bring smiles to others gave me the fuel to practice more.

MY FIRST PAYING CLIENT

"I don't know what I just let go; I'm just very happy that I let them go!" exclaimed Den, after our first sound bath session, which was a case study for my Level 3 in Quantum Alchemy Sound Healing course.

"I am very happy to hear that you have let go of something. There is no need to know what they are. Just know that they are ready to be released," I happily assured him.

"So, how do I sign up for the next session? Can I come weekly? How much is each session, and do you have a package for it?" asked Den excitedly.

Finally, I was able to facilitate a session that helped another person release what needed to be let go. This is what I have been training for: to help others feel what I felt, to release with unconditional love from the Universe through the alchemy crystal singing bowls.

Nowadays, when I travel, I bring a few bowls with me. Intuitively, I know where and when I am to play. Mostly, I play as a sound offering to the land and the sentient beings there, especially when I travel to power spots around the world.

THE TOOL

Sound healing has existed since ancient times. For thousands of years, people have used sound frequencies to help realign the body with the frequencies of the Universe. The sounds from the bowls not only work on our bodies, but they also work on animals and the land.

Why did I choose the alchemy crystal singing bowls from Crystal Tones as my tool for sound healing?

The way I see it, I have the best of three healings, namely crystal healing, sound healing, and color therapy. The healing starts from the moment the participants set their eyes on the bowls. The colors of the crystal bowls are very soothing and help them to calm down. As we all know, different crystals have different healing properties, so when added to the sound healing session, they increase the healing process with their properties.

Let's take the Larimar bowl, for example. It's an F-note bowl and light oceanic blue in color, as I mentioned earlier.

Larimar, as a crystal, is said to help with emotional healing, relieving stress and emotional pain. Although it's usually associated with the throat chakra, emotional healing is linked to the heart chakra. When these emotional healings happen, the heart chakra starts to balance and open.

The beautiful light oceanic blue of the Larimar often reminds people of the calm ocean, bringing calmness, relaxation, and peace. Blue also gives a vibe of stability and reliability that many people who have suffered loss or betrayal crave for.

The F note is the heart chakra frequency. When we play this note, we help to balance and charge up the heart chakra. Hence, when all these three healings are combined in the bowl, it brings calmness and relaxation for the participants while healing the emotional pain they're holding.

Before each session, I set up the room with soft lights, and mats to lay down with cushions and blankets to keep the participants comfortable. The gentle scent of rose and cypress greets them, many of whom would have come from a hectic workplace or rushed through heavy traffic to get here. Then, I check with each of them if there are any specific issues they want to look into. My bowls let me know intuitively the sequence and ways to play. I may play a certain bowl more than others, depending on the situation at that time.

To begin, we take a deep inhalation and sigh out the stress in us. We do this three times. The alchemy vibration of the Larimar starts to fill the room while they relax on the mat, getting comfortable. The gentle vibration of aquamarine gold joins in, cocooning us from the outside space and time, allowing us to dive deep inwards.

WHAT CAN YOU DO IF YOU DO NOT HAVE AN ALCHEMY CRYSTAL SINGING BOWL OR HAVE NO ACCESS TO A PRACTITIONER WHERE YOU ARE?

USING OUR VOICE

During my younger days, I disliked the sound of my voice. Through my spiritual learning, I began to accept my voice and learned to love it. You can start to heal your heart with your voice.

As the saying goes, "Think before you talk." Our voice is a very powerful tool. We can use it to hurt or heal. There are two simple exercises you can do with your voice daily to lift your mood and vibration.

Exercise one:

During music lessons in school, have you sung *do, re, mi, fa, so, la, ti*? This exercise requires you to sing only *do, mi, so*. Try it. These three notes have happy vibrations and help lift your mood when you sing them continuously. I usually do this for about five minutes. You may do it for as long as it makes you feel good.

To ensure you get the right frequency, you can download free tune checker apps. I have listed the notes for do, mi, and so.

- Do is a C note
- Mi is an E note
- So is a G note

For those who are familiar with music chords, this is C major. For me, major chords have a lighter and happier feel. In this exercise, you have to sing the words *do, mi,* and *so* as words also carry frequencies and the power comes from the combination of the word and note.

Exercise two:

This is the first time I'm sharing this personal exercise with anybody. During my younger days, I was traumatized when I sang for others. I started to overcome this trauma with the basic technique of humming. It does not matter what tune I'm humming, it could be my favorite song, a tune that keeps playing in my mind, or a tune that comes from my heart.

From humming, I progressed to singing. I sang from my heart. The tune was familiar, and yet I hadn't heard it before. There were no words, just vowels and sounds. However, I felt my tears falling and my heart opening. Singing is part of my tool now. I sing to the land when I travel with or without the bowls. It's my way of connecting with it.

When you sing from your heart, the tune may not be familiar to you, or the words may sound like gibberish. You don't have to understand what they are. Let them out. Your heart will feel lighter as you release what is ready to be released.

The steps are as follows:

1. Take a deep inhalation, and when you exhale, sigh it out loud through your mouth. Do this three times, it will help to relax your mind and body.

2. Exercise one is a good start to wake up your voice.

3. Sit comfortably and start to hum. You may do this softly if you fear others may hear you. This is a time to put your mind in the back seat. There are no right or wrong answers. Even if the tune you're humming is monotonous, it's still a tune.

4. Continue to do steps one to three until you feel there's a tune that wants to come out from your heart. This can take days or months; it doesn't matter.

5. When the tune is ready, you'll sing it out naturally. I recommend you record this so you can hear them later.

6. You don't have to do this exercise while sitting. I do this when I take a hike, walk home from work, or cook dinner. It always makes me feel wonderful and at peace.

EMBRACE THE NOISE AROUND YOU

Many of us are so busy with our lives in these modern days that we tend not to notice things or sounds around us. I'm guilty of this as well. Nowadays I spend some time just sitting quietly, embracing the sounds around me. It's not easy, for there is always some noise that irritates us.

Explore and reflect on why these emotions are rising within you. Take some deep breaths and exhale slowly as you do that. After a few breaths, check in with your body. How does the noise affect you now?

I find that when I do this exercise, I can tolerate noise better.

I like my environment to be quiet, and I used to be irritated by the noises around me. However, that's not possible in the big city where I live. To be frank, there is no completely quiet place unless you're in a soundproof room. Even then, you'll still hear your own beating heart. So, I learned to be one with the environment. Below is a channeled message when I was thinking about how to talk about environmental noise.

> *Darkest hour, quietest moment. Breathe in, you can hear yourself taking a deep breath in. Breathe out; you can hear the exhalation as the breath escapes through your mouth. Listen, you will hear your heart going "Thump-thump, Thump-thump." The darkest hour, the hour before dawn, is also the quietest. Just as you are listening to your heartbeat, you may start to hear a bird chirping in the background. Softly in the beginning, slowly getting louder. From one bird to a flock of them. Then, a car passes by, splashing a pool of water in the pothole. You are not alone. As you open your eyes, you see a crack of light shining through the darkest sky. The new dawn has arrived.*

I want to close my chapter with this message. It is not only about the sounds of the environment that surround us. It's also to let us know that even when we think we're in our darkest hour, we're not alone. We're never alone—our guides are always with us. They're there for you, waiting for you to see them when you open your eyes.

There is a free heart-opening sound healing video and a chakra-balancing sound session video available only to readers of this book. You may email me or send me a DM on my Instagram for the downloads.

Angeline Poon is a Quantum Alchemy Crystal Bowls practitioner and is one of the first in Singapore to complete the Quantum Alchemy Crystal Bowls™ (QACBP03). She helps receivers release stress, tension, and emotional pain through the sound of the crystal bowls. With the sound of the bowls, she also helps to release blockages in the body and align the chakras with the Universe frequency.

Since the loss of her father in 2018, Angeline has been learning various tools that will help others heal from grief and loss, deal with emotional pains, and release blockages in the body. Besides being a sound practitioner, she is also an ordained Mary Magdalene Priestess, a Violet Flame Rescue Healing practitioner, and a Divine Feminine Reiki practitioner and has completed her AQH01 - Arcturus Quantum Healing® Course Level One by Yantara Jiro.

Angeline provides one-to-one sound healing sessions, group sound healing sessions, and sound healing with Myrraphore's oil and Violet Flame Rescue Healing. She loves to travel, especially to power spots in different parts of the world, and loves cooking and baking, and learning different spiritual modalities that speak to her soul.

If you wish to connect with Angeline, she offers a complimentary 30-minute Zoom meet-up to discuss how she can work with you on your struggles, needs, or vision of the moment. You can reach out to her by emailing her or sending her a DM on her Instagram page.

Connect with Angeline via her Linktree account: https://linktr.ee/thebluemoonstone

CHAPTER 8

USUI REIKI

CREATING A MASTERPIECE
FROM THE BROKEN PIECES OF YOUR LIFE

Carolyn Nicholson Fowler,
URMT, KRMT®, NREMT-P, CRCC, CMRM

"Nothing Changes if Nothing Changes"

~ Donna Barnes

MY STORY

In 2009, my older son died. Then I lost my job. Then I lost my home. You want to talk about broken? I could barely put one foot in front of the other. Now let me tell you how I came to realize each of these occurrences happened for me, not to me. The saving grace? I discovered Reiki and devoured everything I could read and research about it.

I literally discovered Reiki at the side of my son's hospital bed, at which time the Reiki master, who was present with his wife, said, "Close your eyes and visualize blue and green flames around him. Those are the healing colors." Well, rebel that I am, I peeked and suddenly realized I could see the energy flowing around him on the bed! That was a first for me, but I paid little attention to it as I was so invested in seeing my son recover. That was not to be, though, and he died five days later.

After going through an agonizing four months trying to heal from his death, I lost my job. I'll explain later why that was a mixed blessing, but I was really low at that point. Losing a child will make you question every decision you ever made, the good and the bad. I felt worse than useless after losing my job. I thought I was as low as I could get, but the Universe wasn't done with me yet. A few weeks later, my landlady called me. "I'm sorry to do this to you, but I need the villa, and you have two weeks to move out." Shocked, I became a walking icon for depression. I loved my little neighborhood; I felt safe there, which is no small thing for a woman living alone.

After going through those awful few months of healing the profound grief of losing my son, I remembered the Reiki master in the hospital, and I called her. Renee answered on the first ring. "I have been thinking about you since Jon passed. How are you doing?" she said. "Well, not so great, actually. Do you think Reiki could help?" She answered, "Of course. I have felt guided to give you Reiki since I first met you! Let's do it!" We made the appointment.

The Reiki session that followed was transformational. My grief roared out of me as if it were a jet engine. She worked on me for only fifteen minutes, and when I sat up, I realized I could finally breathe! That was the beginning of a new life for me, though I was unaware of how many beautiful changes it would bring. I jumped into learning all about Reiki as if my life depended on it. And it did.

Then I lost my job.

There I was, my son had just died, and I lost my job managing a store (I hated that job!). On the way home, a feeling of terrified freedom hit me. I was so relieved to be away from that toxic atmosphere, but: *How will I make money?* My Virgo brain went into overdrive.

I should apply for unemployment; maybe sell some things. Maybe even try to get back into the medical field.

I was able to get a job quickly doing home care. A proud former paramedic, I now fixed lunches, did laundry, and vacuumed, pushing me farther away from the medical practice I wanted and making me feel even more depressed. But the studying and practice of Reiki took me out of that world for a little time every day. Reiki and the promise it brings for healing and self-worth kept me going. Just barely hanging on emotionally and financially, I applied to some of the many medical offices in the area. Reiki gave me the gumption to think I could challenge the Registered Medical Assistant exam and get licensed—and I did! I was hired into a wonderful office, working with one of the best doctors I've met. His kindness, and sense of humor got me through more than he will ever realize, and the great nurses I worked with rounded out my new work family. It was at this point that my landlady told me I had two weeks to move. Her daughter was fighting with her husband and needed a different place to live. I looked at the heavens and thought: *Seriously?!* I looked for a place in my neighborhood and luckily found one close by.

Through all this chaos, Reiki kept me steady. *What is this amazing healing modality that's having such a profound effect on my life?*

The word Reiki is comprised of two words: rei, which means universal or divine, and ki, which means energy. Reiki Shiki Ryoho has its roots in Japan in the late 1800s and was started in its current form by a man named Mikao Usui, who was born in 1865 in the village of Taniai. In 1870, Taniai did not have an elementary school, so the children went to a temple school (Terakoya) instead, as was common at that time. It should be noted this school was not intended to turn the children into monks or nuns but was the beginning of Usui Sensei's Buddhist education. Sensei means teacher or mentor.

At age 57, after a varied life with many careers such as journalist, social worker, prison counselor, and Shinto missionary, Usui was increasingly frustrated with life, feeling he hadn't yet found his purpose. So, he went to the top of Mount Kurama, a holy site, in 1922 and proceeded to fast and meditate for 21 days. On the last day of his inward journey, he was struck by something like a lightning bolt in his head, and he became unconscious. When he awoke, he felt more energized and alive than ever before. This was his first time experiencing Reiki. After he attained enlightenment, he came down from the mountain, excited by his epiphanies, and opened a dojo to teach the spiritual and healing modality which is Reiki.

The next year, in 1923, there was a catastrophic earthquake in Tokyo, and Usui and his students went down into the city and healed people on the spot. The interest in Reiki burgeoned, and soon, Usui Sensei opened a larger dojo and clinic in Nakano.

Reiki is energy healing, and practitioners build the skill of sensing or feeling energy densities (Hibiki) with their hands. We utilize byosen scanning (scanning with our hands above the person's body). Byosen is Japanese for 'sick accumulation,' which perfectly describes what we're looking for! When we find energetic densities, it indicates a stagnation of energy, which means the energy flow there is sub-optimal. The simple explanation is that we get the energy freed up and moving again, so the flow is back to being optimal for health.

Reiki works on every level: spiritual, emotional, mental, and physical. When clients come for a Reiki session, they come as a complex collection of issues. Most of us are aware we're walking around with emotional and physical issues, but we're usually less aware of the spiritual and mental issues, which is where a lot of our problems start. Reiki, coming from the highest realms for only the highest good, knows exactly what to heal first and can never do harm.

Reiki gently guided me to a deep understanding of myself and life during a time of chaos. It was at this point, about seven years after my son's death, that the uniquely Japanese concept of Wabi-Sabi was brought into my awareness. Wabi-Sabi can be said to embody the most essential of Japanese principles; that the beauty of anything lies in its flaws. As Reiki is a study of balance, so is Wabi-Sabi a study in contrasts, and says that to embody perfection, there should be an equal amount of imperfection. *Could things that were broken and put back together with love be, dare I say it, even better than before? Can people? Even me?*

Yes, I'm happy to say it can be. Reiki was putting me back together, piece by piece, into someone I'm proud of. My practice became more sacred, my students thirstier for knowledge, and my life turned around. How was losing my job a blessing? Once I found work that could pay the bills, I put much more effort into my Reiki development, and my growth in that area was off the charts. I started getting more and more clients, and my classes were filling up. Synchronicities started to show up in life—being in the right place at the right time and meeting the right people; doors were opening for me. I started teaching at the local Technical Institute that had an Adult Community Education Department and more people came into my life! I found that if you meet life with a "Just say yes!" attitude, great things can happen, and did!

How was losing my home a blessing? I moved to a different neighborhood, and all the people around me became family. We all weathered the pandemic together with compassion and humor.

And last but far from least, how was losing my son a blessing? About ten years after he passed, a friend of mine put me in touch with a wonderful lady who is an intuitive. I had accessed intuitives before, but this experience was so light-filled and holy; it was filled with truth that resonated through my soul. She told me, "Your son had many exit points written into this life, but he chose this one because it was time to catapult you into your purpose."

That purpose, for me, is Reiki—the teaching and the healing of it. Then she said one more thing that nailed it for me. "You have done the same for him in another life." Do you know what I mean when you carry a vague unease about something but can't really put your finger on it? That was the answer I was waiting for, that my beautiful son chose to help me in this way, by introducing me to Reiki. You can't make this stuff up!

You are magnificent. Your beauty shines through all that you see as broken pieces and imperfections. You are so loved, whole, and worthwhile.

THE TOOL

It's incredibly important to ground these days. With the chaotic energies swirling around on this planet right now, we recognize calmness as a superpower. I'm going to leave you with a short meditation to help ground you when you begin to feel off-center and frustrated. We begin with some breathwork.

Inhale to the count of four. Hold for a count of four, then exhale for a count of four. Do this three times. You should already be feeling more relaxed!

Close your eyes and picture your favorite tree. Put your hands out and imagine feeling the bark. Connect to the energy of this tree; it's so solid, calm, and strong. You're tapping into that strength and calmness. Now, envision roots growing out of the soles of your feet. These roots are going deep, deep into the Earth. Feel the Earth welcome you with her sweet energy. Send all your anxiety, fears, and pain down into Mother Earth. Gaia will transmute all that negativity back into light. Your roots are entwined with those of the tree. Feel the calm sweetness enter your body from the Earth and the tree. Stay with this knowing for as long as you can.

Now, pull up into your feet all that the Earth is giving you. Let this sensation fill you with loving energy. As you disengage from the tree roots, you notice what is around you without opening your eyes—sun on your shoulders, birds singing, a breeze wafting through your hair. Breathe in for a count of four. Hold the breath for a count of four, and exhale for a count of four. Open your eyes. You have just energetically restarted your day!

Carolyn Nicholson Fowler is a Usui Reiki Master Teacher and a Karuna Reiki® Master Teacher, Certified Medical Reiki Master, Founder of the Peaceful Healing School, and owner of Peaceful Healing Reiki LLC. She teaches all levels of Intuitive Reiki, from Level One to Master Teacher, and Karuna® Reiki. A former paramedic and doctor's office medical assistant, she brings a wealth of medical knowledge to her practice of Reiki. Carolyn is a medical intuitive and channels angelic messages for clients. She partners with a local no-kill animal shelter, Satchel's Last Resort in Sarasota, Florida, to teach animal Reiki. She is available for speaking engagements for groups about energy healing and griefwork.

A good friend of the late Raven Keyes, who authored The Healing Power of Reiki and Medical Reiki—A Groundbreaking Approach to Using Energy Medicine for Challenging Treatments, Carolyn became a certified Medical Reiki Master through Raven Keyes Medical Reiki International and is mentioned in the Medical Reiki book.

Reiki is the gentle, powerful, intuitive energy modality that balances and relaxes the body so it can heal itself. It helps with sleep, anxiety, grief, pain relief, PTSD, and too many more to mention. Carolyn practices both hands-on and hands-off Reiki, described as relaxation for the soul. Carolyn brings the study of Reiki to you with passion, humor and fun!

You can reach her through her website:

https://peacefulhealingreiki.com

Instagram: https://www.instagram.com/carolyn17325

Facebook: https://www.facebook.com/carolyn17325

Email: carolyn17325@gmail.com

I want to share with you how I came to know about Wabi-Sabi:

Hunter, Cheryl, "Wabi-Sabi: The Magnificence of Imperfection" at TEDx Santa Monica, 2013: https://bit.ly/44syH7h

CHAPTER 9

AWAKENING THE VIOLET FLAME CHAKRA

CLEAR, TRANSFORM, AND FULFILL YOUR HIGHEST POTENTIAL

Diana Savil

"I've worked with the Violet Flame before."

"Me too, but I think this is something bigger."

It was.

MY STORY

The hall smelled like all other school halls, musty, institutional, impersonal. The butterflies that danced in my stomach were the same as years ago, at school speech days. Yes, this was all horribly familiar.

Relax. You're not at school now. This is not the same. You're an adult, and this is a workshop. You might be learning, but this is different, and something special. Trust it.

An excited murmur ran through the room as our presenter stepped onto the stage. Edwin Courtenay, healer, channel, musician, artist, and more. I'd heard about him for some time; today, at last, I got to experience his teaching. The event was channeled to Edwin by the Ascended Master Saint-Germain; I'd been working with him for a while.

No wonder I have butterflies, this is going to be a very special occasion.

I settled in for the ride.

As Edwin began his introduction to the Violet Flame Chakra and what it offered, I felt the buzzing in my hands which indicated a shift in frequency. My third eye chakra began to pulse as my head became light and spacey. I felt myself open to energies beyond the everyday.

By the time he invited us to experience the first stage in the Violet Flame Chakra Awakening process, I was well away:

Unaware of the physical space, sensing only the energy around and within me. Lost in it, held, somewhere beyond the physical. His voice seemed to come from far away; I was in my own universe surrounded by and filled with the most amazing energy.

Somewhere within it my consciousness registered:

Violet. All Violet. Everything is Violet . . .

". . . making your way back." Edwin's voice summoned us. I returned, blinking at the mundane surroundings. Slowly connecting more strongly with the physical once again.

More was to come. The Violet Flame Chakra Awakening process itself—moving even deeper into the energy, and experiencing a profound shift: in energy, in frequency, in *everything*. Transported to another realm, another space. And returning knowing that something deep and powerful had occurred, which would irrevocably change my life.

And it did.

The next few days were somewhat dreamlike as I gradually adjusted to the change in my energy. Everything felt different, as if I was viewing it through a prism of radiant light. I still plodded through the mundane—the washing up, laundry, cooking—but I felt my body moving through subtle changes, not tangible enough to put into words, but there, for sure.

My breathing rhythm altered. I felt vital, alive. My physical body zinging and tingling, and an awareness, all the time, of something new, different, beyond myself, in the ether around me.

As we met for our weekly walk, I had to share my news with Alison.

"It's amazing! There's this star you learn to create using the energy of the Violet Flame, and you can do so much with it!"

"Like what?"

"Well, you know the Violet Flame transmutes negative energy into positive energy—doesn't just clear it like other processes do, but actually changes the negative into positive?"

"So you lose the negative energy and get positive instead?"

"Yes!"

"Cool!"

"Well, the star is made of that energy. So if you put yourself in the star, anything negative that comes near the star gets changed into positive energy before it can reach you."

"Wow!"

"And because all the energy inside the star can only be positive, it means you are totally surrounded by purely positive energy!"

"So can you use the star for other things, as well as putting yourself inside it?"

"Yes! That's what's so amazing! As well as putting myself in it every morning, I've put it in each room in the house, round the car, round the village—even round the whole Earth!"

She laughed. "We certainly need it!"

"Yes. You can use it for situations too, and people, and objects—anything you can think of."

"I want it! Can anybody have it, or just healers?"

"No, anyone can have it. And once you've had your own Violet Flame Chakra Awakening, you can awaken other people's chakra so they can use the star too. There are other tools as well, but I haven't used them yet. The whole thing is wonderful."

I promised my Saint-Germain group I'd share the Violet Flame Chakra Awakening with them at the first opportunity. As we got nearer to our next meeting, I felt my nerves. The process of channeling his energy and his words was familiar, and suddenly seemed really easy compared to what I now faced.

As my breath quickened, I gave myself a talking-to:

You can do this! Come on, it's the same people, in the same space as every week. They'll all be supportive—you'll be fine! Okay, this time you have to present someone else's work and carry out a process you haven't done before, but you can do it. You know you can.

And as my heart rate began to settle, I remembered:

I can put the whole thing inside the star!

And I did.

I felt the energy shift, my shoulders relaxed, and I breathed easily.

Of course I can do this. It will, indeed, be not only fine but wonderful. How amazing to be able to do this for others. I am blessed to have such a gift.

And it was fine! It was amazing to pass this process on to my loyal friends, and their response at the end of the evening was more than I could have hoped.

"Thank you, Diana, that was amazing."

"Thank you for such a wonderful experience."

"I am blown away by what I just felt."

I was on a high as we drove home and resolved next to use the Violet Flame Rescue Healing tools that were another gift of the Violet Flame Chakra Awakening process. As often happens, when we make a decision to move forward, Spirit responds fairly rapidly!

It was just a few days later, during a Reiki treatment, that I felt guided to use one of the rescue flames—tools of the Violet Flame Rescue Healing—that were now accessible to me.

My client was deeply relaxed already, eyes closed, hands uncurled; lost, I thought, within the Reiki energy.

Without moving my hands or stopping the flow of Reiki, I began the process of calling in a rescue flame.

I had an idea of what to expect, but I did *not* expect my client to suddenly say "Wow!" at the exact moment that the rescue flame energy flowed in. I smiled to myself as the treatment continued.

Afterward, she was eager to speak.

"That was incredible! What did you do? There was suddenly this amazing energy everywhere, and I feel so different. Clearer, cleansed. What happened?"

I laughed.

"That was Violet Flame Rescue Healing. I used one of the rescue flames. They work on different levels—the usual: physical, mental, emotional, and spiritual—and reach more deeply than most other healing energies. They can clear away residue from old conditions that have been treated with other techniques but have left a residue. The rescue flames can clear that away."

"That fits! I felt completely immersed in the energy, as if it was filling every part of me. And I do feel completely different: all bright and shining, like I've been polished!"

We laughed.

At her next treatment, she had hardly sat down before she was enthusing about her change:

"I tell you, I feel like a new person! I can see everything clearly—it was in a kind of cloud before—but I can see now what's important and what isn't. They've even commented at work.

"It's a transformation. I can't thank you enough. It's that amazing Violet Flame Rescue Healing, it's magic!"

My Saint-Germain group was also exploring the gifts of their Violet Flame Chakra Awakening, and all had similar positive tales to tell.

"My client had her first full night's sleep for years. Her mind was clear and calm."

"We'd been working on a condition for months with no change. Within two weeks it's suddenly improved!"

"I notice the difference when I put myself in the star to meditate. Everything is much deeper, and I get such clear guidance."

I, too, found magical changes as I brought the Violet Flame Chakra gifts into my life. As I brought the star into being around me each morning,

I felt ready to face the day. I called in the Violet Flame Rescue Healing flames to support my healing treatments, and profound changes took place within my clients. I used the rescue flames on myself, too, surrendering to the full power of their cleansing energy and noticing the benefits.

Word spread about the experiences of my Saint-Germain group and my clients, and people asked if they could receive their own Violet Flame Chakra Awakening. Saint-Germain himself was also prompting me to share the process, and so I held what was the first of many Violet Flame Chakra Awakening workshops. I followed Edwin's original format, and the energy of the Violet Flame Chakra was spread further.

The responses continued to be the same:

"Amazing."

"Transformation, on a deep level, thank you."

"My life changed for the better since the awakening."

And there were some other results too:

I had a vague memory that during my own Violet Flame Chakra Awakening, mention was made that the process might "ignite your potential," but I gave it no further thought.

As students shared with me what unfolded for them in the days or weeks after their Awakening workshop, I began to realize that this, too, was one of the gifts of the Violet Flame Chakra.

A rise in personal vibration, certainly, as any other initiation process. And an increased sensitivity to subtle energy; again, to be expected. But what was also being reported were things that weren't obviously connected to the spiritual—recognizing, of course, that everything is connected, and the spiritual permeates all.

Other results included unexpected and spontaneous weight loss within a short time, inspiration about a new career path and individual teeth communicating with a dental surgeon as to what treatment they did and did not want.

Will I experience the same? I wondered.

The morning after one Awakening workshop I picked up a book someone left behind. I can't remember the content, but what I will always remember are the thoughts that came as I read.

This is written in really large print, spaced out. There are only 100 or so pages—not many words at all. And yet it looks like a proper book. You could write something like this. It would be quite easy. You could do it.

As I read, I became more aware of the excitement growing within me. Waves of energy rippled from head to toe. My hands tingled. My head buzzed with new thoughts.

A book. I could actually write a book. This dream had always been far off on the horizon, in the distance, but within view. Now, suddenly, it was becoming possible.

The book in my hand was abandoned as I allowed the thoughts and energy to flow.

I could actually do this! I could have my own book! See a book with my name on sitting on a shelf! Have people buy a book that I have written. This is amazing!

The subject matter was without question: It would be about the Violet Flame Chakra, the means through which I was brought to this magical moment in my journey when a long-held dream that once seemed so far away, was about to become a reality.

I was going to write a book about the Violet Flame Chakra!

And I did.

It was a challenge, of course, as all growth-enhancing experiences are, and a much more complex process than it seemed on that inspired sunny morning, but it was accomplished. *Awakening the Flame* was published in April 2015, and continues to sell. I shall never forget the sense of pride and achievement as I held the first copy in my hands, shaking a little with the enormity of the moment.

And my writing career is unfolding further, with my contribution to this book.

Another writing project—again spontaneously manifested by Spirit—is also underway, and I sense there will be more to come.

My teaching and healing work continues too, but the writing aspect is clearly part of the potential ignited through my Violet Flame Chakra Awakening. One of the many gifts that that amazing process has given me. I will always be grateful.

To find out how you can experience your own Violet Flame Chakra Awakening visit:

https://www.violetflamechakra.com/violet-flame-chakra-events/

And to purchase your copy of *Awakening the Flame:*

https://www.amazon.co.uk/Awakening-Flame-Igniting-Potential-through/dp/1504327888

THE TOOL

The Violet Flame can be invoked to transmute negative energy into positive energy.

Anyone can call on it, with no need for training or initiation. It has been used in this way for centuries.

In itself, the Violet Flame is a powerful tool for transmutation. With the gifts you receive at your Violet Flame Chakra Awakening, you are able to connect more deeply to its energy and to direct it in more ways.

CLEANSING WITH THE VIOLET FLAME

The Violet Flame itself can be used to cleanse:

• Yourself

• Someone else

• An object, e.g. crystal

• A space

• A location

• A situation

• Food before you eat

• The energy after an argument

• Any negative thoughts you have

• Whatever you can think of

The process is simple:

• Have in mind the destination/focus where you want to use it.

- Say: "I now invoke the Violet Flame of transmutation."
- Visualize violet-colored fire moving through whatever it is that you want to cleanse: yourself, the space, a crystal, etc.
- Give thanks for the gift of the Violet Flame.

This process can be called on quickly and easily, in any situation, and is a useful tool to have in your toolkit.

CALLING THE VIOLET FLAME INTO YOURSELF TO TRANSMUTE NEGATIVITY

This process can be experienced as a meditation, allowing yourself time to be immersed in the energy of the Violet Flame.

Settle yourself comfortably, either sitting or lying down.

Close your eyes and take a few slow, gentle breaths.

Allow your body to relax: drop your shoulders, unclench your jaw, breathe deep into your abdomen.

Ask that the energy of the Violet Flame may flow into you, cleansing all negative energy.

Feel the violet-colored fire begin to move through you.

Allow it to cleanse your whole being, every layer of your energy field, every cell of your body.

Feel the energy of the Violet Flame, seeking out all negative frequencies and transmuting them into positive ones.

Become aware of any old, negative emotions that no longer serve you, and ask the Violet Flame to transmute them, clearing and cleansing them from your system.

Surrender any physical aches and pains to the power of the Violet Flame, and allow it to burn them away.

Allow the energy of the Violet Flame to clear from your whole being all that does not serve. Release it, let it go.

Know that only positive energy can remain in the powerful vibration of the Violet Flame.

Stay in the energy for as long as you wish.

When you feel ready, slowly bring your awareness back to your physical body and the physical space in which you are.

Ground yourself by consciously connecting your energy to the Earth beneath you.

Take your time to return fully; rub your hands, wiggle your toes. Drink some water to bring you back into the physical.

THE VIOLET FLAME AS A TOOL OF ILLUMINATION AND INSPIRATION

Saint-Germain told us back in 2019 that the Violet Flame was originally used as a tool of illumination and inspiration. Through necessity, it became used as a tool for transmutation, but the intention was always to return it to its original purpose when the time was right. He told us that the intended process of return was now beginning.

During a Violet Flame Chakra Awakening workshop in February 2024, he told us we should focus consciously on the Violet Flame as a tool of illumination and inspiration, as well as a tool of transmutation. This would help to strengthen the illumination and inspiration aspect of the Flame, as it continued to grow.

PLACING YOURSELF IN THE VIOLET FLAME TO ILLUMINATE AND INSPIRE

Settle yourself comfortably, either sitting or lying down.

Close your eyes and take a few slow, gentle breaths.

Allow your body to relax: drop your shoulders, unclench your jaw, breathe deep into your abdomen.

When you are relaxed, visualize yourself walking into a temple.

In the center of the space is a large, sacred fire, burning with a Violet Flame.

The fire is cleansing; it will not burn you. It is a Violet Fire of illumination and inspiration.

Slowly, you move towards it.

When you are ready, step into the fire. Stand in the center of the vibrant flames.

Feel yourself immersed in the energy.

Feel it flow through every cell of your being, illuminating, inspiring.

Feel yourself filling with light, radiating light.

Open your awareness to new ideas, new inspiration.

Allow yourself to receive, to become illuminated and inspired.

When you are ready, step out of the Violet Fire.

Turn and give thanks to the fire, to the energy of the Violet Flame.

See yourself leaving the temple and slowly returning to the here and now.

Ground yourself by consciously connecting your energy to the Earth beneath you.

Take your time to return fully; rub your hands, wiggle your toes. Drink some water to bring you back into the physical.

Diana Savil has been working with energy in various forms for over 30 years.

She is a Usui Reiki Master and former teacher of Setsukido, a deep tissue/Ki massage technique. She has studied crystals, aromatherapy, and hand reflexology.

For many years she worked with the Ascended Masters, particularly Saint-Germain, channeling their words and energy for clients and in groups.

Tarot was her first venture into spiritual work and through the years she has continued to read for clients, and to teach Tarot courses.

She has presented workshops on a wide range of subjects: crystals, channeling, the Divine Feminine, Higher Frequency Chakras, Atlantean Light Symbols, Ancient Avalon, and more.

She has been working with the energy of the Violet Flame Chakra since its inception in 2013 and set up the associated website, as well as writing *Awakening the Flame,* charting the early days of this work. She regularly carries out Violet Flame Chakra Awakenings, for individuals and groups, and has also presented The Lady of Silver workshop, a further stage in the Violet Flame Chakra energy.

Over the years, she has led many meditation and spiritual development groups and taught a variety of courses. She regularly gives Usui Reiki Attunements, at all levels.

She has recently returned to working with the Galactic Beings after a 20-year gap, bringing through their energy in healing treatments and guidance readings.

She is a channel for the light and introduces light transmissions and higher light codes into her healing and teaching work.

Having tried to retire in 2021, she now lists working as one of her hobbies—allowing her to continue to do what she loves. She also enjoys reading and walking in the countryside.

Connect with Diana: https://linktr.ee/diana_savil

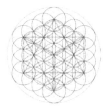

CHAPTER 10

ACUPOINTS

TURNING TEARS INTO JOY

Tove Kirsty Lewis

MY STORY

In a split second, I made my life's most important decision. I am taking it all in; I can breathe. I'm going to move to a warm climate. I was 13 years old on a four-week health trip to Igalo, Yugoslavia in 1987.

My siblings were excited to listen to my mum's sounds and screams during the night. They stayed in bed all night even though they couldn't sleep. They waited many months for this. It came as a shock to my mum; I was not planned at all. A winter night in 1972, my mum pressed me out from her womb in the bedroom next door, a normal home birth in those days. There were no falling stars when this Capricorn was born.

Seven different chronic disabilities, all well-hidden, would turn up in the most unexpected combinations and varieties of symptoms. They were often incompatible, too, giving me heaps of challenges. I hated all of my disabilities /illnesses/ diseases for preventing me from living my life how healthy people did—going out among people, eating all kinds of food, playing with animals, and using public transportation without getting ill.

Hate will not get you anywhere; it is self-destructive and sabotages healing.

I discovered the benefits and knowledge of having all these disabilities. By welcoming their lessons in life and not hating them, I helped myself heal. Now, I call them my chronic friends, a technique I use with my clients for their processes.

My mum stopped breastfeeding. Boom! Out of nowhere, a few started showing up, sincerely uninvited.

I wasn't even a toddler when I had the pleasure of becoming acquainted with the hospital for the first time—breathing problems, allergic reactions, eczema, and a small body full of medication. When I got older, other new chronic friends were discovered; they stayed permanent and multiplied with symptoms.

My blue, itchy, runny eyes didn't see what they should. Training and patches didn't help; glasses became a new daily outfit. My left side looked like the bottom of a Coca-Cola bottle on top of the nose. I had pale white skin and two rows of small rotten teeth, revealing a story in itself.

Kids were incredibly creative in finding names for me because of all my invisible friends they knew nothing about; they even thought it was contagious and couldn't come out and play. Their parents were scared of asthma and allergy in the eighties. I wish I could say we don't need to create awareness now in 2024.

I could've joined the circus, putting my legs over my shoulders and walking on my hands. Hyper-mobility can look fun and entertaining. It's totally the opposite. My sixth friend (diagnosis), a permanent one, was discovered at age 17. Every school I went to assumed it was my illnesses, medication, trembling hands, and a long list of other issues that caused my bad marks and struggle to read and write.

You'd think one of my teachers was the genius I needed. No way, guess who it was? A man who received a few letters from me, a secretary in the local asthma and allergy association. He was the national leader.

"You need to be tested for dyslexia."

Eureka!

The seventh problem reared its head—learning languages at school other than English and Norwegian, which we always spoke at home. I had difficulties beyond having dyslexia. I was tone-deaf and sang flat/false half-tones. With an unfamiliar sound, learning certain new words isn't the easiest task in the world.

At certain times, my friends are very visible, and a whole symphony orchestra is coming from my lungs. I can go from Beauty to the Beast in seconds, depending on reactions to a wide array of allergens. Over the years, I became worse—hyper-allergic, hypersensitive, and suffering from severe asthma. Giving a hug to other people or a kiss on the cheek gave me a rash. I reacted to what my partner ate through his body fluids, and I was allergic to latex.

Western medicine played a huge part in worsening my health as I was diagnosed with several new chronic friends and given more medications. In the end, it wasn't all new illnesses. There were also new diagnoses based on symptoms of the side effects of the medication. They even wanted to do surgery, which I chose not to have (with a 50% chance of becoming better). My body reacts badly to anesthesia. I didn't dare take the chance.

Intuition and knowledge of the rareness of reactions I'm used to having weren't common to doctors or specialists. I've saved my own life more than once. I often wonder how many extra years I've spent in bed, isolated from a normal social life, unable to do anything physical.

In the last years of the 90s, I was headhunted to be a guinea pig, one of seven people to test a new higher education for people with disabilities. In the second year, newbies started up. There, I met Echo, a beautiful soul. We became good friends—a human friend, not a "chronic friend" like the others I mentioned earlier.

I put in all my energy and effort to succeed. I had two degrees down the drain because of being hyper-allergic and having asthma. I couldn't take it anymore; I had to do what was best for me to survive.

Like me, Echo didn't choose the easiest life contract either. We both had severe challenges with health. I talked passionately about wanting the freedom to heal, including my plans how to earn my own money online. The most important was a decision I made in former Igalo when I was 13—to move to a warm climate to heal. Joyfully, it turned out we had several interests in common.

One magical day, Destiny, Echo's husband, invited me to join them on a vacation to the south of Europe. They had a small house not far from the coastline. I couldn't resist. I felt something calling me. This was a new start to our long journey together, a piece of land where I found my own paradise on Earth.

We both searched for answers, trying out all kinds of treatments and methods. We longed for cures for our separate conditions. Unfortunately, there was no scientific breakthrough in time to save a damaged body. Echo, may your soul rest in peace.

I'm very rich—not financially, but in gratitude to life itself—waking up every day! I have a unique superpower combined with a sense of dark black humor. I don't give up. Every time I fell hard and was totally crushed, I found a solution. Thirty years of Western medicine failed; oh yes, I'm alive, but with what quality?

Traditional Chinese medicine became a big turning point for my recovery and path, leading to self-healing, and this is why I have so much to offer people. I reduced most of the 12 different medications I depended on daily. *No, how could I forget?* There were a total of 14 medications when I was extra sick, plus more if I needed antibiotics.

Years of treatments and a lot of effort turned into a new profession, training and working hands-on with doctors and therapists, where I started as a client.

Holy shit! Who would have dreamed the magical and mysterious universe would lead me to these perfect moments? Our paths have crossed in the most beautiful and worst possible ways. I'm over the moon, breath-taken. There's no coincidence; everything happens for a reason; it only depends on the choices one makes and the consequences of the outcome.

Something was stroking my left hand like a cold breeze. It was Echo from the other side, finding a way to get through to Destiny, through me. I called Destiny, and he was flabbergasted and touched. *Time to let go, create space for love to re-enter, and experience new adventures.*

He wished he could find a way to heal the wounds and communicate with Echo himself. I wanted to help him, but he was so far away, so I thought of a way for Destiny to start his process here and now.

It took some time to digest the information given by Echo. As a result of that, my senses became stronger, and other abilities opened up. After my near-death- experience on a hot summer day in 2019, I hadn't officially come out of the closet with my new opportunities to help myself and other people.

Echo and I are now distant from each other, turning tears into joy and laughter by accessing the power within. The grieving and shallow breathing for over a decade is now gradually transforming into something amazing that'll show when it springs out in full bloom.

I guided him on where and how to use fingertips-pressing on acupoints, combined with meditation, to visualize the goals. Acupuncture points open up blockades to give free passage, balancing the qi and letting energy flow. Session by session, I provide more tools to work with.

Dear Destiny, Echo, your beloved partner and soulmate, my friend, is always around us. Vibrating on high frequency, in a higher dimension. Not solid, not liquid, just in a different density.

Destiny, fly high and far, and spread your wings now that you can communicate and heal from the inside out.

THE TOOL

Traditional Chinese medicine (TCM) approaches the body in a holistic way—physical, psychological, and spiritual as one. It aims at prevention by maintaining a balance of yin and yang energy to allow qi (vital energy) to flow and heal disease.

TCM has several practices; one of them is acupressure, where I use the description of acupoints and the use of fingertips to stimulate specific points located along the meridians. Acupoints have many benefits. One is to release the body's natural painkillers and affect areas in the brain involved in processing pain. Meridians are channels that form a network in the body where the qi flows.

What we don't remember, our soul, subconsciousness, body, and cells remember. This includes everything we've ever been through—the positive, laughter, joy, and happiness, and the negative, trauma, pain, and tears. The negative influences create stagnation and unbalance in yin and yang preventing the qi flowing through all the meridians. When blocked, pain or illness occurs. Positive influences can release the good hormones, and help to restore balance.

We need to get to the root of what causes the symptoms we want to heal from and treat the main issue, not only the symptoms.

TCM was very useful for me as a patient in my healing processes, so I could start to work and practice several disciplines. I include other modalities for each individual, depending on what their energy tells me. I guide people through how they can utilize acupressure on acupoints using their fingertips or other blunt objects.

The acupoints to use:

GV 20 (Crown Chakra Opening)

This powerful spiritual point on the crown of the head, located in the center of the "soft spot" on an infant, can be used to open up and balance healing energy. The GV (Governing Vessel) 20 is particularly relevant when it comes to opening the light field energy. Connecting to GV 24.5 opens up inner spaces for a direct pathway to the soul.

GV 24.5 (Third eye)

A powerful acupoint for the pineal gland and re-balancing. The GV 24.5 is located in the middle of the forehead between the eyebrows. This acupoint is also where light enters the skull to activate the pineal gland, an important anatomical location. Stimulated in the right way, combined with breathing techniques, it can balance and give physical well-being, and open up to spiritual perception of the world and the universe!

Process of Acupressure:

Reserve time just for yourself, where you won't be disturbed. Make yourself comfortable; sit or lie down. Start by placing your hands on your belly under the belly button and feel your breathing. Inhale deep through your nose as far as you can expand your belly, and hold for a few seconds, exhale slowly through your mouth. Repeat this at least three times.

Make sure you continue to breathe with your belly; do not raise your shoulders and become tense.

Use the middle finger to press the acupoints. Begin first with gentle pressure, then add more, and hold with a steady touch. You can add pressure as you go. Start with a few minutes, and build up to a maximum of ten minutes on any acupoint. Focus on breathing energy into them.

Silence your mind; feel where there is tension. Let go of every thought that pops up. If you become emotional about any difficult feeling, take three new deep breaths, continue to breathe normally, and focus on silencing the mind and letting go whilst pressing the two acupoints.

Drink water after every session. Let one to two days pass between every session you do.

I'm **Tove Kirsty Lewis**, a mixed breed, born in the UK, raised in Norway, spending periods of the year in the south of Europe. I was born with seven hidden, chronic disabilities. My life was isolated and challenging—a martyr, a word I understand the meaning of too well, whilst seeking justice and acceptance.

I was, and still am, given a different perspective and abilities to solve challenges from the universe my way. All my education, including four degrees and years with volunteer organizations, helps me work on all levels for people with disabilities. And years of working with TCM give me a huge advantage for my future plans.

I went from birth and a life full of trauma, pain, and tears to turning it all around to something positive. Hell on earth became my earthly Heaven.

The raw life journey and choices I made helped me fulfill my life purpose to change the world, in how we know it today. I'm building up my charity company and organization with teams of volunteers and spreading it around like a dandelion, spreading its seeds and growing in spite of it all.

I'm manifesting we collectively raise the vibration and frequency of Mother Earth to love. I aim to create awareness and educate the leaders in Western medicine. We need to treat our bodies holistically; all is energy. I want my life suffering to mean something to the disabled and my story to give hope to people to find their inner power to self-heal and create the life they want.

www.tovekirstylewis.com

tkl@tovekirstylewis.com

www.inspiteof.eu

CHAPTER 11

RAPID TRANSFORMATIONAL THERAPY

RELEASING FEAR WITHIN

Sofia Pereira, Clinical Hypnotherapist

MY STORY

And just like that, the mind was still, the body was calm, and life had a new look. The nights before school were happy; the whole family enjoyed dinner together, and bedtime was calm and pleasant.

This wasn't the case for eleven-year-old Tristen at first. He woke up in the morning with his stomach hurting. He couldn't eat breakfast, felt lightheaded, and had a very noisy mind with horrible looping thoughts.

The nights were just as bad; he wasn't sleeping well and just kept on thinking about the next morning. He started to be absent from school because he felt so bad he couldn't make it. As time went on, he stopped going altogether, and it started to affect his sports, family, and social life with friends.

His mother, Bernadette, took him to his pediatrician, a gastroenterologist, and a neurologist, and every test came back normal. Nothing was medically wrong with Tristen, yet his life turned upside down.

Bernadette reached out to a psychologist and spoke to his school for help. Tristen attended sessions with the psychologist, and the school started a reentry program, which included a school psychologist meeting him at the front door and walking him into the school. He went to their office, and when school officially began, he proceeded to class if he could or stayed in the office doing work.

This carried on for two months, and Tristen wasn't getting any better. In fact, he wouldn't even make it to school, and on days he did get in the car to go to school, just looking at the school from the car made him worse, and his mom had to drive him home.

Tristen just wanted to be home; that was his safe place, where he felt good. Bernadette didn't know what else to do or where to take Tristen for help. She just knew her child was suffering and needed help. But what was causing Tristen all these emotions and symptoms? What happened to cause his life to spiral out of control?

A friend made a suggestion. "Why don't you try Rapid Transformational Therapy Hypnotherapy?" And they referred her to me. She called me to explain Tristen's situation. "Can you help him? He isn't sleeping well at night, worries about the next morning, and when he gets up, he feels sick. He won't eat breakfast, and if he goes to school, he won't eat lunch."

Bernadette continued to explain that schoolwork was piling up, adding even more anxiety, and that he was losing weight and living in fear. She said the school was trying to help, but some days, no one was outside waiting for him, and she'd have to call the office, making Tristen more anxious.

I agreed to see him and chat to explain how I worked and what he'd need to do if we agreed to work together. While talking, he kept saying, "I can't tell you what's causing this. I just want my life back."

I assured him, "You don't need to know what caused this. Your subconscious mind holds all the answers, and in no time, you'll know and begin to get your life back." His Mom scheduled a session; he looked very optimistic and excited.

Tristen arrived for his session wearing a Portugal soccer jersey with Cristiano Ronaldo's name on the back, black shorts, and white Adidas sneakers.

He was nervous; his eyes darted around the room, scanning my bookshelf; he fidgeted with his fingernails.

"I will help you relax deeply, and we'll investigate your memories. By speaking to your subconscious mind, we'll get our answers," I explained.

He lay on the couch and began to relax, listening to my voice, and let everything go as I started the induction to relax him even more.

I took him to a space where the logical brain goes to sleep, and the subconscious brain awakes; in this relaxed state, I returned him to the place, event, and time where this same feeling (anxiety) showed up for the first time in his life.

As I asked him questions, he replied with certainty. I constantly assured him he was safe, "You're just visiting this scene from the past and not reliving it." I took Tristen to three different scenes in his past that caused the symptoms he felt.

In scene one, Tristen was in his fourth-grade class, started to feel unwell, and threw up. His classmates made faces and laughed at him.

"It smells!"

"This is gross"

Tristen felt embarrassed, made fun of, and out of control.

In the second scene, at school at recess, his friends made fun of him, which made him feel alone, sad, and mad that he has no control over other people's actions.

"It makes me feel sad. They are calling me names and telling my other friend not to play with me."

In the third scene, he was in fifth grade, and his group of friends excluded him. One friend persuaded the others to exclude and ignore him. This made him feel alone, sad, and anxious.

"I feel so alone and confused because I'm a great friend, and this is not fair. Why are they acting this way towards me?"

These three scenes showed me that Tristen felt he lacked control and had developed emetophobia, causing an overwhelming, intense anxiety about vomiting.

How did something that happened two years earlier cause these issues?

Change often causes trauma to resurface.

Tristen was in fourth grade with a regular schedule of going to school, with sports after school and on weekends, and then Covid hit.

Everything shut down, and no one had the answers to when life would get back to normal. School was on Zoom; the whole family was home, and it felt scary but safe at the same time.

The family was together all summer as his parents worked from home, and in September, Tristen entered senior year fifth grade; school was only in session two days a week, with three days hybrid. Finally, in November, when school reopened for five days, if you encountered someone in the classroom who had COVID-19, you'd have to be quarantined for ten days. Back to school on Zoom for ten days, back at home feeling nice and safe.

Masks were finally not mandatory until April, and his senior trip and graduation were right around the corner. Goodbye to elementary school, and hello to middle school.

September comes around, and it's a new school, middle school, with new friends to make and new teachers to meet. Tristen felt overwhelmed, unsafe, and not in control.

These feelings of not being in control caused anxiety, making him live in the future and worry, worry, worry.

The 'What-ifs' started to pop up more and more often until that's all he thought about. What-ifs became looping thoughts.

As we continued our session, I asked Tristen, "What's the role of this part in your life?"

The part said, "To keep him home because it's safe."

I asked Tristen, "What is the intention of this part in your life?"

The part said, "To protect him, keep him safe."

I asked Tristen, "What's the purpose of this part in your life?"

The part said, "To keep him home because it's safe."

I asked Tristen, "What's the intention of this part of your life?" The part said, "To keep him safe."

Anxiety was present to protect him by keeping him safe at home. No one could make fun of him if he was safe at home. If he threw up it'd be okay because he was safe at home. And no one can make him feel left out if he's safe at home.

We now knew the cause of his presenting problem, and how it manifested for him.

I was able to reframe those beliefs for Tristen under hypnosis.

I reframed them deeper still by recording an audio that Tristen listened to for 21 to 30 days.

In my work with children, I talk about anxiety as a cockroach as a way for them to differentiate themselves from bad thoughts.

The cockroach in their mind (anxiety) is just a liar, a voice trying to keep them still and feel bad.

While listening to the recordings each night, Tristen would try to go to school each morning, and some days he stayed all day, others a half-day. Little by little he began to feel better.

He started to go to school every day but still had some additional work to do with emetophobia. On our second session, I didn't need to regress him as we knew the cause of the anxiety and instead spoke about the thoughts and feelings he experienced. I made him another recording focusing on the emetophobia and learning to trust his body.

He listened to it for about two weeks and then just like that, the mind was still, the body was calm, and life had a new look. The nights before school were happy, the whole family enjoyed dinner together and bedtime was calm and pleasant.

It took Tristen less than six weeks to be his old but improved self. He's been thriving in school, sports, and life because he has coping tools and knows that it's just a cockroach lying to him in his head.

He knows that he's safe in school, has a voice he uses to tell others how he feels, and that there is always someone to help, so he knows he's not alone.

When I work with a child/teen, I also work with the whole family, as it affects everyone. Through gentle, empathetic therapy (hypnotherapy) sessions, I work to transform negative beliefs and fears into positive affirmations and confidence. Imagine the negative thoughts as cockroaches—pesky, persistent, but ultimately powerless when you shine a light on them.

I help your child squash these cockroaches and replace them with empowering beliefs.

Rapid Transformational Therapy (RTT) harnesses the most powerful healing potential on the planet: your mind. RTT is based on the science of neuro-plasticity and combines the most beneficial principles of hypnotherapy, including psychotherapy, Neuro-Linguistic Programming (NLP), Cognitive Behavioral Therapy (CBT), and neuroscience that works with both the conscious and unconscious mind and gets to the root cause of the presenting problem.

Everyone is different, yet it works for everyone. The client heals what they're going through themselves, learning to let go of any baggage, guilt, shame, abandonment, etc., and loving themselves more.

THE TOOL

The tool I'm gifting you will enable you and your child to relax and release negative thoughts and feelings.

Imagine hovering just above your head is a little hurricane of energy. There is a vortex of pure, healing energy hovering just above the top of your head. And this little hurricane is moving in a clockwise direction, from left to right. It's wider than your body's widest part—it's slightly wider than your shoulders, it's slightly wider than your hips. And this hurricane of energy is very soon going to enter your body and move right through your body, keeping it well within its sphere.

As it moves through your body, it's healing, repairing, and regenerating anything that needs it. You can see this hurricane of energy moving from left to right. And now is the time to heal. You can feel the tail, the very tip of the hurricane, just touching the top of your head as that healing hurricane moves into your body.

It's moving into your head, erasing any bad thoughts, stomping on that cockroach that keeps lying to you; it's shining light on the truth, the truth about how lovable, and calm you are and that you're safe. It moves into your ears, erasing any untruthful words you've heard or caused you pain. It's moving into your eyes, taking away any bad visions that have left pain.

As it moves into your body, all of your energies are realigned to match the energy of this healing hurricane. It's moving down, moving into your throat. Your throat is an area related to emotions, and as this healing hurricane moves into your throat, it is slowing down. It's slowing down and doing all the healing work that needs to be done. It allows you to have a voice. You can speak beautifully, you can speak in front of groups, you speak up, you speak out, you have a voice. What you have to say makes sense and matters. This healing hurricane is slowing down in this area of your throat and rebalancing, repairing, and revitalizing everything to do with speaking, swallowing, and even digesting.

Now, this healing hurricane is covering your shoulders. It's moving down further into your body, moving down to your chest, slowing right down as it begins to cover your heart. As this healing energy covers your heart, it's doing the most profound, the most healing work. It's erasing, eliminating, and removing any heartache, pain, old hurts, issues to do with rejection or abandonment, or feeling not lovable or not enough. They're all wiped away as this healing energy vortex slows down and covers your heart.

This healing energy is rather like a broom. As it moves through your body, it gathers in front of it any toxic feelings, substances, or anything that shouldn't be in your body, including any toxins, but also any toxic thoughts or memories left in your heart, mind, throat, or stomach.

They're moving ahead of the healing energy hurricane, soon to be moved out of your body forever. This healing energy leaves your heart open and happy—open to healing love, knowing you're lovable and that you're enough. You always have been; you certainly always will be that away.

This healing energy moves down through your ribs, balancing, repairing, and strengthening. It's focusing on your spine, making your spine so strong. Your spine is your support system, and as this healing energy balances your spine, it balances, soothes, and helps all the muscles around your neck.

Now, this healing energy is moving down through your lungs, balancing your breathing. You breathe properly, you breathe in, you breathe out. The healing energy is moving into your stomach, taking away any trapped pain and emotions. Just let it go.

Your body feels more perfect and alive, because your metabolic rate, your metabolism is becoming perfect. That healing hurricane of energy is now moving from your shoulders down to your upper arms, down to your forearms, and down to your fingers. Feel your fingers and palms tingle as they let go. That healing energy is moving from your stomach into your hips and moving from your upper back to the small of your back as every muscle and nerve feels strong.

That healing energy, as it starts to move out of your stomach, moves in front of it every toxin, stuck emotion, and bad feeling that shouldn't be there. They're pushed ahead of the healing hurricane, being shoved out of your body.

And now that healing hurricane is moving down through your legs so that everything that doesn't belong in your mind, body, psyche—anything, any imprint, impression, memory, imperfection, any hurt you no longer want to be in your life—is being pushed ahead of this healing hurricane.

You feel that old stuff moving down toward your knees and calves. Your calf muscles feel incredibly heavy as the healing energy starts to move down to the soles of your feet. And I want you to imagine you're opening a valve in the soles of your feet, and all that stuff is coming out, so all the sand starts to tip out, pour out, and drain out. You can feel this kind of sand pouring out of your body, tipping out of your body, taking out everything that shouldn't be there.

And while you feel the sand trickling, pouring, and moving out of your body, you feel amazing. You feel relaxed, calm, and full of confidence. In just a minute, you're going to slowly, easily, calmly come back to full awareness, absolutely knowing with unshakeable confidence that you've experienced an extraordinary transformation and that you have everything you need in you, feeling wonderful, feeling healed, feeling amazing, feeling extraordinary.

Because that is the truth about you.

Play this recording a lot, because you respond to it amazingly. And every time you play this recording, feel the last remains of that heavy sand dropping out of the soles of your feet. Feel that valve in your feet closing. Everything is new and healthy, shiny and perfect. You're feeling liberated, free, healed—so extraordinarily healed, phenomenal, incredible, proud of yourself, and good about yourself.

Open your eyes, fill up your lungs, and slowly, calmly, and easily come into full awareness. And, of course, when you play this recording at night, you can drift into the deepest, healing sleep that will carry you right through to your normal wake-up time. And you can do that any time at all, including right now.

You can pick up a free recording of my tool at

https://sofiapereirahypnotherapy.com/

Sofia Pereira is a Clinical Hypnotherapist and practices Rapid Transformational Therapy (RTT). She specializes in children/teens with anxiety, depression, and phobias. She is a member of I.A.C.T (International Association of Counselors and Therapists), where she continues to grow by constantly seeking new modalities for kids/teens' anxiety, depression, and phobias. She was born in Portugal and immigrated to the US in 1988, learned English and worked hard to attain the American dream with the support of her family.

Neuroscience and Psychology interested her from a young age, and she decided to pursue a career in Hypnotherapy. She is a wife and a mom to four beautiful kids: Sofia (15), Skylar (8), his twin Scarlet (8), and Saige (7). She is your normal quintessential PTA mom, a Girl Scout Troop Leader for many years, and is driven to help kids/teens.

She believes as a parent we should fight to preserve the innocence and happiness of those precious formative years of childhood/teenhood. She is accessible worldwide through Zoom and locally at her office in New York. You can get free resources, knowledge, and support by following her on;

Facebook: https://www.facebook.com/SofiaPereirahypnotherapy/

Facebook Group: Parents of children and teens with school anxiety and school refusal: https://www.facebook.com/groups/344535859250009

Instagram: https://www.instagram.com/sofiapereirahypnotherapy/

Sofia's website for free resources, audio, and booking sessions: https://sofiapereirahypnotherapy.com/#

CHAPTER 12

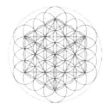

FYRE PHOENIX

RISING FROM THE ASHES OF PAIN
TO YOUR DIVINE ESSENCE

Kimberly Barrett

MY STORY

Oh No! Not right now. This can't be happening!

I grip the steering wheel of my car so tightly that the muscles in my hands begin to ache. I back off the gas pedal and glance quickly at the rearview mirror, trying to cope with what's happening.

Okay, Spirit, I know I said I wanted to see energy with my eyes open, but now? You could have picked a better time!

Relief that no one else is on the road at this time of night is the only thing keeping me steady. Before my eyes is a large orb, swirling with various shapes and colors like a kaleidoscope. The center of it is transparent enough just to make out the road in front of me.

My heart is filled with fear and wonder. My mind races a million miles a minute as thoughts rapidly overlap one another.

Is this really happening? Will I make it home safely? What is it I'm seeing? It's so bright and pretty! Maybe it's an anomaly from the streetlights hitting the windshield.

My eyes frantically dart around to determine the source only to have the orb move to stay centered in my line of sight.

Okay, keep calm, deep breaths. This is happening. Just two more miles to go. I can do this. Please, angels, get me home safely!

Parking behind my building, I feel my shoulders begin to relax, and tension starts to leave my body. Closing my eyes for a moment, I exhale the breath I didn't know I was holding in.

Thank you, angels, for getting me home safe and sound.

I open my eyes to see the orb still in front of me outside the car, as if waiting for me. I feel a sense of urgency to get inside my apartment as quickly as possible.

Oh, God! Something big is about to happen.

Making my way to my apartment, my curiosity grows as the orb stays with me even at the elevator. My hands tremble slightly as I take out my keys.

I wonder if John has gone to bed already. I wonder if his being in the room will alter whatever is about to happen. Will it affect him in some way?

I open the door to see my husband watching something on the History Channel. "Hey, Sweetie. How did practice go with your students tonight?"

"Things went great. There were a few questions and good healing sessions all around. I'm just going to sit on the couch and decompress before going to bed. You know how doing energy stuff at night has me supercharged for hours afterward."

"Okay, I'm just going to finish this episode and then head to bed myself."

While talking with my husband, the orb moves into the living room as if waiting for me to sit on the couch. Once I do, an unexpected surge in my energy field puts me on full alert. I begin to assess what I'm experiencing at all levels of perception. The center of my chest begins to tingle as my heart chakra is flooded with energy. Alarms go off in my mind.

Wait a second here! Is someone going to tell me what is going on first?

Part of me rises up, trying to stop whatever is going on, and another part wants to see where this goes. Confusion sets in.

Do I want whatever this is to happen? It doesn't look like I'm getting any answers. I'm not feeling anything negative from it. I can't control this or understand it, so do I allow this? Would it be that bad to see where this goes?

Reaching through the fear of my ego, that little voice that while trying to protect me also keeps me from moving outside my comfort zone to grow. I comfort that part of me saying, *I know you want to protect me. Let's see what the angels have to say about this. You know they never steer us wrong.* I take a breath into my heart and ask my angels what to do.

Just go with it. Don't fight it. You know in your heart this is sent from up above. Trust us. Trust the process. More will be revealed in time.

Relaxing into the next breath, the tingles in my chest intensify as my heart chakra expands. Before I can take the next breath, I feel the same tingling sensation begin in my hands and extend out until it feels like I'm holding a large plate in each one.

All the while, my eyes are glued to the orb as it continues to spin. There are colorful flashes of blue, red, green, purple, and yellow, making patterns I've never seen before and yet somehow feel familiar. As soon as I grow accustomed to what I'm seeing and feeling in my body, the orb suddenly comes at me, landing on my head like an astronaut's helmet. My systems and brain become overwhelmed as they're flooded with more energy than they can hold. Pressure begins building in my head, seeking release and not finding any.

As the pressure continues, my crown chakra explodes out in all directions, and my head feels numb as if given a lidocaine shot.

I know I don't have eyes outside of my body, so how can I see laser beams of light shooting out from the orb to different parts of my brain?

The impact of each causes momentary discomfort, which I imagine would be much worse if not for the prior numbing. I can only conclude it's an energy surgery of some type, a rewiring and download, though I've never experienced any of these to this magnitude.

I don't know how much more of this I can take! Please finish quickly. I know I gave my permission, but I had no idea it would be like this.

The entire process comes to a sudden and complete halt. The energy around my head feels as though a balloon popped, and everything within rushes out, yet it doesn't go beyond my auric field.

Rest, and we'll help you integrate this while you sleep.

I look at the time on the cable box, thinking only five minutes have passed, but I'm astonished to see twenty-two minutes have elapsed! As I groggily rise from the couch to get myself to bed, I feel as though I've just completed a triathlon wearing a full suit of armor.

* * *

The following days, weeks, and months found me repeating this process at odd intervals, often in the safety of my home, with the occasional unusual appearance. The most profound one occurred during a class I taught.

"Breathe out through your feet, growing roots deep, deep, deep, into the Earth–grounding yourself. When you're ready, relax and open your eyes."

"That was an amazing activation meditation," my friend and student, Maureen, said with a smile.

"Everything about this healing modality is just over the top, and I love teaching it. Let's take a few moments and let that settle before we move on."

I feel a shift in energy in the room which signals I'm about to have another orb visit. The hair on my arms stands on end, and it feels as though every cell in my body is vibrating.

Why am I shaking like I've had two pots of coffee?

"What's going on?" asks Maureen. "The energy in the room has shifted, and you look like you're in shock."

"Remember those orb visits I told you about in our group practices? One appeared, and it's starting to work on me." My body is no longer relaxed in the chair; I sit fully up with my body rigid. I keep reminding myself to take full, deep breaths, but the rest of me doesn't get the memo as I keep catching myself holding my breath.

"You don't look very comfortable right now."

"It really isn't, but I'd rather have it be quick and uncomfortable than long and drawn out."

"Do you think I can touch it?"

I take a moment to feel into the question and mentally ask the orb, now sitting on my head, if it can be touched by Maureen. "I'm not getting a 'no' or a negative feeling around you touching it. Go for it."

"Where is it now?" Maureen asks as she scans the area.

"It's around my head and is about two feet wide."

With arms extending out in front of her, I watch Maureen's hands begin to touch the outer edge of the orb. She quickly snatches her hands away, flicking them like she's trying to shake off whatever she feels. "Oh, my goodness! I've never felt anything like that! How can you even sit there in it? Not that it was bad; it was just so powerful. No wonder you're uncomfortable."

"I do my best to hang on until it's done, go about my day, and then rest to integrate. I wish they'd give me the instruction manual already. I'm ready to know how to use these downloads."

"Well, let me know when you figure it out."

"You'll be one of the first people I tell, for sure!"

* * *

I take out a notebook and place it beside me. Grabbing my water bottle, I take a refreshing sip as I begin to set my intention for my weekly meditation. I sit in silence after asking a question and listen for the answer. I feel as though I've run out of ways to frame the questions I have about the orbs. I choose to ask, "Who is going to help me understand what has been happening?"

It's been two years since the first orb visited and I feel no closer to gaining insight than I did then. I take a few breaths to clear the frustration I'm feeling. I sit in silence waiting for a reply. In my mind's eye, a man appears before me. His warm eyes smiled as much as the rest of his face. He reminds me of Jesus, but I know he isn't. Before I can analyze any further, he begins to speak.

Are you ready? It's finally time to work with what we've been giving you. We've been preparing you to work with energies that haven't been available to this planet before. You are to be a bridge for these energies. To help yourself and others reach beyond the physical and opening to dimensions where the purity and channels of light are available to assist in reprogramming the cellular systems to restore order, wholeness, and balance. To remember, reinitiate, realign, revitalize, and reconnect to the soul's purpose and truth. This expands the soul's ability to transverse time, space, dimension, and reality to enable living a life without boundaries or limits. My name is Master Kuthumi, and I look forward to being the first of many to assist you in this endeavor.

I hastily jot down what I receive before it escapes me.

* * *

Understanding deepens as I begin to bring in these new energies to my healing sessions. I'm able to work with these new energies and witness how quickly my clients now overcome obstacles holding them back and heal from things they've been holding on to for a long time. My client Pamela is the best example of what Master Kuthumi explained about what the energies, now called Fyre Phoenix, can do.

"Pamela, so how do you feel now after your session?"

"It blows me away every time. I think I come in for one thing and get something else so much deeper than expected. I can't believe my life now. I'm a completely different person than the one who walked into your office all those years ago. I can't believe all the shit I've let go of from living with tick-borne disease and the mental and emotional damage that it caused. I feel held in such a sacred and loving space each time to let it all go and come through to the other side. It's like I've been cracked open, all the yuck has been scooped out, I'm grounded, and in touch with my heart. I'm excited to be alive again!"

"I have enjoyed watching you come alive again. Gone are the days when you came through the door looking defeated before we even began. Now I see the endless opportunities just waiting for you to step up and into them. When you're ready to start learning how to do this healing for yourself, let me know. You've graduated, so to speak, and really only need to see me for energy tune-ups or if something challenging comes up."

* * *

I humbly thank Master Kuthumi, Angel Aurora, St. Germain, my longtime mentor and friend Julianne Santini, Aeveia, my Spirit team, my soul family (you know who you are), my students, my clients, my husband and Creator, who all believed in me when I felt lost in grasping what was being gifted to me.

Fyre Phoenix is a very versatile healing modality. It can stand on its own, or the tools within can supplement and amplify other energy healing practices. Taking the course greatly accelerates one's spiritual ascension journey. The practice I offer as a tool is just one of many taught in the course.

THE TOOL

We often view ourselves as the personality trapped within the body our soul wears. We're so much more. We're created by a magnificent source, which most of the world identifies as God. The purpose of this meditation is to tap into the power of your soul—your divine essence—and own it. It's designed to assist you in breaking free of the chains that bind you from life, society, family, and even yourself–the outdated thoughts/belief systems, emotions/feelings weighing you down, and pain/trauma in any form at all levels of your being, physical, emotional, mental, and spiritual.

Give yourself time for this experience. Ensure there are no distractions. Make yourself comfortable, preferably sitting. Your intention and focus are all that's necessary for this process. Repeat daily for optimum results.

Before you begin, ask that your angels, higher powers, and/or God, surround you and protect you during this experience.

1. Close your eyes and take a few deep yet gentle breaths into the center of your chest, where your heart chakra is. Take any chattering thoughts and expectations and put them in a bubble. Place the bubble off to the side for now.

2. Take a few more deep yet gentle breaths into your heart chakra with the intention of connecting to the spark of the Divine within you. This is the place containing the true essence of who you are. Feel the power and pure love held here.

3. With each continued breath, allow this divine spark to expand. Allow it to expand in all directions–up to and including your throat area/chakra and down to and including your solar plexus area/chakra.

4. Feel how the power and pure love now radiates out like rays of the sun. You may even envision it as a sun with bright golden white light shining forth.

5. Now, focus on or call forth any troubling thoughts or emotions. It can be feelings of unworthiness, stress about a project, anger, or whatever you choose.

6. Send them into the blazing sun, and watch them dissolve in the flames of your divine essence.

7. Call on your next thought or emotion. Send it into the blinding light of your divine essence and witness it dissolving. Keep repeating the process until nothing comes forward.

8. Continue to focus on the light emanating from your divine spark, and ask to feel the love of your soul, your divine essence, fill you and wash away anything untrue. Take your time, and allow this for yourself.

9. Then, feel the love, light, and power of your divine essence filling every cell in your body. The spaces between the cells. The mental, emotional, and spiritual aspects/bodies of yourself. Feel the strength and the power of who you truly are.

10. Take a breath into your heart chakra and send a beam of love and light out through the soles of your feet, anchoring all of this goodness into the heart of Mother Earth.

11. Finally, send a beam from the light of your divine essence and project it out in front of you with the intention to send it into the day ahead of you—to continue to walk in the light, love, and power that's the highest expression of who you truly are.

12. Ask your guardian angel to seal this love and light around you. Ask for their help in integrating this love into your body to heal what's needed with grace and ease. Give thanks to your soul and any angels who aided and assisted.

13. Take a few moments to become aware of the body. Wiggle your fingers and toes. Open your eyes when you're ready. Don't rush off to do the next thing. Allow yourself to be present. Once you feel grounded, gently move into the rest of your day.

I encourage you to keep a journal to capture your progress. You'll find that with continued practice, life opens up with grace and ease that wasn't present before. You engage with life from a place of power instead of running or hiding from it or sitting on the sidelines. Visit my website to get a free recording of this meditation, book a remote Fyre Phoenix session, or sign up for my next Fyre Phoenix class.

Website https://www.lightuponthelotus.com/

Kimberly Barrett has over two decades of experience helping people heal. She receives wisdom from angels, ascended masters, and spirit guides, and draws heavily on Violet Ray energies. Kimberly is the originator of Fyre Phoenix, a healing modality designed to free you from all that is holding you back from standing in the divine perfection that you are.

Kimberly practices and is certified to teach Melchizedek Method, Magnified Healing, Integrated Energy Therapy (IET), Karuna Reiki, 5th Dimensional Bodywork, and various crystal therapies. She is certified to practice Spiritual Coaching, Brain SOULutions, Bars (Access Consciousness), Shamanism, and Tong Ren. Kimberly melds the lightness and mysticism of fairies with the intensity of the violet flame.

She is a big believer in the healing power of nature and has been known to whisper to flowers and trees and hear their guidance. Some even say with her pointed ears, she is an Elfin herself. Kimberly communicates with crystals and has developed innovative, new therapies from the wisdom stored in the stones. When not assisting clients or teaching, she can most often be found with her nose in a book, coffee in hand, and her cat Luna by her side.

If you find yourself in Manchester, New Hampshire be sure to visit Kimberly's practice, Light Upon the Lotus.

Website https://www.lightuponthelotus.com/

Facebook https://www.facebook.com/profile.php?id=61558397892406

CHAPTER 13

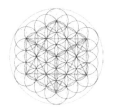

SECRETS OF SEKHEM & VENUSIAN WOMB WISDOM

WILD INSTINCTS UNCHAINED FOR INNER TRUTH & SENSUAL LIBERATION

Nydia Laysa Stone, Somatic Healing Artist, Therapist & Coach

MY STORY

COME TO THE TEMPLE — SACRED RITES OF INITIATION

Get off your knees, my daughter!

Come over here and look in my eyes!

Her commanding voice resonates within me and sends a shiver through my spine; her presence and raw energy pulsating through this tiny dark temple, captivating my senses. She's so alive in here, so physical!

I step in front of her, feeling shy within her powerful field, but she reminds me:

Sister - don't play small!

Remember who you are! Never forget we are equal!

Sekhmet appeared in my intuitive artwork, meditations, and dreams for a long time.

She was the one calling me away from the peaceful life in my little Caribbean paradise during my 4 am New Moon Eclipse ritual.

Fly with the winds and dance the dragon lines!

Come here to meet me in my chapel!

That's how it started, this spontaneous, crazy journey, my guided spiritual quest that would lead me halfway around the planet and through sixteen countries in sixteen months.

GOOD GIRLS RUNNING WITH THE WOLVES

You might think, *who's this crazy lady, imagining Goddesses talking to her?*

Or maybe they're communicating with you, too! And you feel it's kind of normal.

Well, for me, it is. I've been open to spirit since my earliest childhood - as we all are as kids.

We all run with the wolves, fly our dragons, dance with spirit, and the fairies until they teach us to 'stop the nonsense' and be a 'Good Girl.'

Our wild instincts are wide awake when we first discover our sensuality. But by that time, they already locked and tied our wolf in cages of beliefs, manners, shame, and fear.

They planted their seeds of doubt and insecurity, carved their guidelines into our bodies and brains, and set our inner radio to a single channel. They indoctrinated their Barbie mindset and taught us what's supposed to make us truly happy.

I rebelled against all of this.

How come?

Maybe a small defect in my wiring? My late husband used to say the fear center in my brain wasn't developed because I was born at seven months.

Or maybe too much oppression? Or too much running barefoot on Mother Earth, climbing trees, communing with animals, elves, and my ancestors, reading 'dangerous' books or poetry.

Whatever caused my rebellion, I looked around and felt:

I don't like what you show me, how you live. You're not truly happy.

I don't want this kind of life you're selling me here!

I allowed my wild child to run free in the jungle, nurtured my primal instincts, and tuned my inner radio to a different frequency to keep out their noise; my senses staying aligned with the elements, my intuition, and guidance - to save myself from becoming trapped and domesticated.

My wild dragons soared me out into the world at a young age, leading me to my destined places and relationships.

Greek philosophers, Freud, Jung, and Anais Nin swirling around my head; I studied Yoga, Tantra, and therapy in India and had a spontaneous Kundalini awakening, meeting Kali in her temple in Calcutta at only 18, which scared the hell out of me!

Fortunately, my Indian community guided me lovingly through my process, and my life took an early turn toward spirituality. I explored sacred ceremonies and healing modalities and worked with street kids, in slums and women's shelters.

I've experienced several encounters and attunements with other archetypes - again, most recently in Peru, Jordan, and Bali on this magical mystery tour.

None of it prepared me for this moment, though, when I finally stood face-to-face with Goddess Sekhmet in her chapel in Egypt!

Electrified by her energy coursing through me, I knew she was calling my soul - and I answered, stepping into the realms of the Divine.

The feeling of homecoming is simply overwhelming and makes me cry like a child from my most vulnerable places within, washing out this old, coarse, hardened pain I didn't even know I had.

Remember, we are equal.

A deep breath widens my chest; my body expands, unfurls, and straightens.

I claim my space, feel all my senses clear, sharpen, and smile into her eyes.

SURRENDER TO THE CALLING

At first, I wasn't willing to follow Spirit's calling!

What? No!! I can't go anywhere right now!

I have construction going here, and no money.

But, as usual, I only receive friendly nods and patient smiles from my guides once they've transmitted their messages to me.

Although this one felt more like an order!

So, now you want me to drop it all, get up, and fly to Egypt?

Beneath my huffing, puffing, and foot-dragging, though, I clearly feel the pull of destiny and sparks of excitement in my gut, the wave of joy that grabs me every time I think of venturing on another exploration.

It's the amphetamine of a lifelong, global nomad!

But there's also an irresistible urgency I sense, a distinct inner knowing lingering: this journey is not just any other trip. This one might turn my world upside down.

I can already taste and smell it - the mystical, the enigmatic! Like the fragrant oriental spices awaiting me in the colorful bazaars, the sacred sites, salt lakes, meteorites - the serenity of the desert.

As much as I love the turquoise waters and lush tropical jungles I chose to call my home base, I do admire the desert.

The clearly defined lines and shapes, endless undulating waves, ripples, and colors, the ever-moving, transforming sculptures, and scenery created by fierce winds and fluctuating lights.

THE NILE!

Lifeblood of Egypt, the watery path of initiations, winding along ancient temples teeming with history, each holding unique light codes and mysteries.

All my favorite goddesses, murmurs, and rustles of papyrus scrolls, pharaohs, sacred crocodiles, and feluccas drifting by.

Aye! Here I go again!

I pulled out my cards and pendulum to ask for more insight into the messages I received in my eclipse meditation, but instead, I opened my phone and searched for flights to Egypt.

Ten days later I lock up my casita, cuddle the cats and horses farewell, and surrender to the calling.

After all – who'd ever dare say *no* to a goddess?

SACRED SITES AND SONGLINES OF THE LAND

Sekhmet, Hathor, and Isis have been showing up in my life for a long time now in symbols, ceremonies, and paintings.

I wrote them spontaneous poems at 3 am, waking from the strangest dream journeys.

Now Sekhmet and Egypt summon me, tugging at old bonds, weaving through centuries and millennia - connections grown in my former lifetimes.

I've already discovered many of these ties in various spiritual sites along the ley lines—mostly intertwined with the remembrance of the land: ancient Minoan temples, Asclepiums in Crete, sacred valleys, canyons, and condors in Peru, caves in Jordan—and of course in Mama India, my oldest friend.

WINDOWS OF MY SOUL

As if time had paused to witness our encounter, her fierce gaze sinks into mine for a silent exchange. She studies me, unraveling my layers with an intensity that leaves me breathless.

My soul lays bare and opens to our connection, fully immersed in her primal force and ferocious strength. She ignites flames like wildfire in me, burning, stripping away the veils of doubt and insecurity that had obscured my perception.

I've been seen.

JOURNEYING BEYOND THE SANDS OF TIME

Still holding her gaze, honoring the sacred bond forged between us, I slowly reach out, gently caressing the black, smooth stone of her majestic form.

She's so much taller than me!

I lay one hand on her heart, the other on mine, and my breath stumbles!

A strong current flows immediately.

Touch my Udjat, now your own third eye,

My eyes, your eyes.

My vision blurs, colors swirling.

Throat to heart, her dark voice, guiding me through the rites.

Solar plexus.

A radiant sun opens in my belly, darkening to glowing orange, then red, heating my womb space.

A deep humming vibrates through me, my bare feet on the old stones, merging with the mother.

My body starts shaking, reminiscent of Kali's serpent moving in me.

QUEEN OF THE DESERT WINDS

Her fiery breath opens wide golden landscapes – shimmering with primeval powers.

Energies like liquid metals rise through my feet and into my womb; the molten heart of Gaia burns out residues of age-old afflictions, flows through my channels, and circles in my throat – the brightest blue!

Speak your truth! she thunders.

The energy travels out of my crown into my eighth chakra, the seat of my soul.

Expanding and melting into timeless infinity, I'm whirling into a journey beyond time and space.

Temples, dancers, flames, wars, and rivers spiral back to visions of ancient cultures, symbols, and ceremonies.

Sekhmet's wild breath sends me through the songlines of my lineage, my connections to Egypt's mysteries.

Remember who you are!

This is the Age of the Feminine!

Her countless instructions and chants keep echoing from the walls of the chapel.

Some I understand, others continue dawning on me still.

It felt as if Sekhmet claimed me as her own, marking me as a vessel for her divine will.

And though I couldn't yet comprehend the full extent and impact of these transmissions, I knew I was chosen for a purpose far greater than myself.

I feel her moving in me ever since these unforgettable initiations; just one deep breath unleashes the untamed lioness, her wild, fierce love and presence, and the codes and blessings she poured into me.

LIFE TRANSITIONS – CREATE YOUR OWN STORY

I have traversed the globe, studying cultures, belief systems, and modalities and channeling the universal language of healing energy frequencies.

In each destination I call home, I invoke the local archetypes, infusing ancient wisdom with the latest neuroscience to craft bespoke retreat experiences, sanctuaries for radical life transitions.

Drawing upon the transformative powers of archetypal energy, I created the concept of the Four Agreements, Rites & Rituals for the Re-Wilding path for women.

They serve as time-proven catalysts, a roadmap to liberation—an orientation amidst the tumultuous challenges of modern women as they reclaim their inner truth, wild instincts, and innate sensual and ecstatic potential.

REWILDING - GOOD GIRLS, VAMPS & WITCHES

So - what's the fuss about these Re-Wilding Retreats?

What do they do there? Sleep in caves?

Actually – if that tickles your fancy - I do offer caves in Jordan, near the sacred site of Petra, one of the 7 Wonders of the World – where I lived in caves with the Bedouin tribes – now my soul family!

Usually, though, I facilitate my retreats with small groups in handpicked, often luxury venues in stunning natural settings; cultural and spiritual immersions in high vibrational locations – my chosen homelands.

In the fluid dance between somatic therapist and seeker, it's my passion and joy to witness women rise and roar, open up and bloom like exotic flowers, vibrant, untamed - with each breath, each movement, rewriting their story, and transforming their raw potential into empowered action!

S, a charming 74-year-old lady joined my latest Re-Wilding Retreat in the ancient Asclepiums of Crete and said:

"Nydia, teach me Tantra! I want to finally love my body and discover my sexuality! I've been a good Texan girl, a mother, grandmother - but always dreamed of dyeing my hair red, being a vamp, a wild witch, and living in Crete."

I admire her courage to fully trust me – and the energy healing modalities she's never heard of! She passionately engaged in Yoga, emotional detox, Tantric and somatic embodiment, passage rites, cacao, and womb healing ceremonies– and even in some of the more intimate, or "woohoo" practices, like soul retrieval.

Under tears of pain and joy, we healed decades of symptomatic physical issues, suffocation, eczema, and oppression on her chest.

She inspired me and I'm thrilled to have witnessed S leaving her good-girl existence in Texas, and alchemizing her lifelong dream into reality!

We stand together as a tribe of wild wise women in our divine power and sovereignty, creating our own paradigms, infused by New Earth consciousness and love.

THE AGE OF THE FEMININE IS HERE NOW.

You can work with me–virtually or in person in my Re-Wilding Retreats:

COME TO THE TEMPLE

and receive the codes directly through the goddesses!

THE TOOL

THE FOUR AGREEMENTS OF RE-WILDING RITES & RITUALS FOR WISE WARRIOR AND MEDICINE WOMEN

I created the concept of Four Agreements and Seven Rites & Rituals for my Somatic Healing Sessions and global Re-Wilding Retreats to support women on their path of healing and liberating their feminine life force energy.

Each rite contains several tools and rituals and can be used separately. Here below, you will find three of these tools you can work with today.

The complete concept of the Seven Rites & Tools is available online, and I'd like to offer it to you as a gift for reading this chapter (link below)!

My profound holistic Re-Wilding process reconnects us to our creativity, sensual expression, passion, and joy.

Sekhem energy inspires this concept. Sekhem is an ancient healing energy used in the temples by the priestesses for thousands of years.

Patrick Zeigler received Sekhem in Giza in 1979 – still the Age of Pisces. The new Sekhem energy frequencies I channeled with Sekhmet in her own temple in Karnak in Egypt hold higher wild woman activation codes to bring forward the Age of the Feminine and New Earth consciousness, and will be registered as a new modality.

THE FOUR EMPOWERMENTS OF THE FEMININE

I. SPEAK YOUR TRUTH WITH INTEGRITY

Liberate your Wild Voice & Authentic Expression

RAW – REAL - BARE

- Healthy boundaries – practice your 'No.'
- Release 'Good-Girl-Syndrome' & societal conditioning.
- Create your reality through the power of word and thought.

II. SOVEREIGNTY – REMEMBER WHO YOU ARE

Authority, Freedom of Choice, Responsibility

I DON'T NEED YOUR APPROVAL

- Self-worth, self-acceptance, self-love.
- No judgment: 'I am enough.
- Do your best - perfect Imperfection.

III. EMBODY FEARLESS AUTHENTICITY

Cultivate Curiosity - Explore and Play

UNFOLD YOUR OWN MYTH

- Courage, resilience, detachment.
- Light-hearted and joyful living.

IV. IN SENSES VERITAS – SENSUALITY AND WOMB WISDOM

Unchained Instincts, Pleasure, and Grace

LOSE YOUR MIND TO RETURN TO YOUR SENSES

- Wild Heart abundance, create moments of ecstasy.
- Hidden rivers rising - Tantric explorations & Divine erotism.
- Innovative muse of intuitive creation.

WILD WISE WARRIOR WOMAN EMBODIMENT

Archetypal energies and their aspects can support you in your practices. Chose intuitively, which Divine being, qualities, and elements to call in for your rites and rituals to serve your intentions.

SEKHMET: Fire - passion, vitality, and purification.

- Represents fierce strength, courage, and protection.
- Power of transformation, healing through fire and destruction.
- Inner warrior - stand in your truth and defend your boundaries.

HATHOR: Earth - grounding, abundance, and fertility.

- Symbolizes love, beauty, pleasure, dance, joy, the feminine.
- Embrace your sensuality - find joy & delight in the pleasures of life.
- Self-love, self-care, self-acceptance, nurturing.

ISIS: Water - flow, intuition, and emotional depth.

- Embodies the divine feminine wisdom, magic, and intuition.
- Archetype of the Great Mother, protection, guidance, unconditional love.
- Compassion, forgiveness, heal ourselves and others.

VENUS: Air - intellect, power of thought, communication, diplomacy.

- Sensuality, pleasure, divine feminine, grace, elegance, beauty, art.
- Archetype of the Great Mother, protection, guidance, unconditional love.
- Physical, earthly aspects of sexuality, self-love, acceptance, relationships.

THE SEVEN RITES & RITUALS

1. RELEASE

2. LET GO OR CALL IN

3. VISUALIZATIONS

4. MIRROR RITUALS

5. SELF LOVE

6. EMBODIMENT

7. REFLECT & INTEGRATE

YOUR THREE SOMATIC RE-WILDING TOOLS FOR TODAY

TOOL A: PRIMAL SCREAM THERAPY

Prepare: a pillow, journal, and water

Set your intention:

- Do you want to release blocked emotions?
- Perhaps connect with your primal wild woman energy?
- What needs to be heard?

Breathing

- Inhale through your nose, deeply into your belly - exhale fully through your mouth.
- Center yourself.

Scream

- Inhale deeply and bring awareness to your body and the present or upcoming emotions.
- Let out a profound, primal scream from deep within you.
- Let your instincts and needs guide you. Observe without judgment.
- Express through writing, art, or gentle movement, best in nature.

TOOL B: THE FIVE SYMBOL MEDITATION

- **Ankh:** life force portal, spiritual power, divine energy
- **Was-Scepter:** authority, power and sovereignty
- **Udjat or Eye of Horus:** protection, healing, third eye
- **Lotus - Sesen:** purity, spiritual awakening, potential
- **Uraeus - Serpent:** sovereignty, feminine, wisdom

All the above symbols are associated with Sekhem energy.

You can meditate with the images, visualize or draw each symbol, and reflect on its meaning and inspiration for you and how you can integrate its qualities into your life.

TOOL C: ANASYRMA MIRROR RITUAL

Inspired by an ancient Egyptian fertility rite: women or goddesses would expose their breasts and genitals to the River Nile, to temples or statues.

Through this empowering practice, you will liberate your wild sensuality and desire, overcome negative conditioning, shame, and guilt, and open up to pleasure, ecstasy, joy, and wild heart abundance.

- Prepare: candles, incense, silky materials, mirror(s). Open intimate sacred space and set your intention
- Slowly discover your body, touching and caressing yourself with curiosity, tenderness, passion, and reverence. Integrate the mirror(s) fearlessly.
- Notice thoughts and emotions arising without judgment.
- Fully explore your sensuality and orgasmic wildness in this sacred space.

- Speak gentle words of affirmation and self-love as you admire your body and close by feeling gratitude for its beauty, strength, and ecstatic potential.

I hope you benefit from these rituals! I'd be honored to support you on your journey, either in-person or virtually.

Find free guidance, meditations, and practices, including an audio of this chapter and tools, tantric yoni arts and retreats at:

https://www.healingartsbynydia.com/sekhem

Nydia Laysa Stone, Somatic Therapist, Life Transition Coach, Bestselling Author, New Earth Visionary and Healing Artist.

Miracles are just a shift in perception

Let's explore your awakening path toward joyful, sensual living and your journey of healing and transformation. Reclaim your power and authenticity through Tantric Embodiment practices, Vision Quest, Shamanic Ceremonies, integrating yoga, art, and neuroscience. Nydia is an experienced master teacher of the Healing Arts, Violet Flame, Egyptian Sekhem energy, Reiki, and worldwide light code activations, Yoga, Tantra, breathwork, dynamic meditations, dance & art expression, soul retrieval, and the Rites of the Munay Ki.

Nydia is passionate about movement in all its forms, overcoming stagnation and catalyzing change toward empowered expansion.

Her signature Rewilding Retreats for Women are transformative experiences: cultural and spiritual immersions in the world's most significant high-vibrational locations, including Egypt, Peru, India, Bali, Fiji, Greece, and the Caribbean Islands – Nydia's chosen 'homelands'. For over 35 years, she has lived, studied, and worked as a global nomad in these inspiring environments.

Based on Tantric and sensual explorations, as well as Somatic embodiment practices, Nydia's curated sessions and retreats will connect you to your inner knowing, innate womb wisdom, and ancestral lineage to awaken the Wild Wise Warrior and Medicine Woman within.

Nydia will guide you through vision quests and passage rites, igniting your life transitions to find alignment, purpose, and focus and initiate sacred shifts and your soulful metamorphosis toward the liberated, joyful, and heart-centered life of your dreams!

You can often find Nydia in canyons, climbing on a rope over waterfalls, barefoot, dancing Salsa on tropical beaches, singing around a campfire, or cuddling some furry friend. She loves elephants, jaguars, and mangoes.

Nydia communicates fluently in English, German, French, and Spanish.

Work with Nydia:

Linktr.ee : https://www.linktr.ee/@healingartsbynydia

Instagram: https://www.instagram.com/nydia.laysa.stone/

https://www.instagram.com/healingartsbynydia/

Facebook: https://www.facebook.com/nydialaysastone

Website: https://www.HealingArtsbyNydia.com

Retreats: https://www.healingartsbynydia.com/retreats

CHAPTER 14

SERPENT HEALING

TRANSFORMING FEAR TO LOVE
BY ACTIVATING YOUR KUNDALINI POWER

Kwali Kumara

"Inside you lives a tremendous power—it is God's greatest gift to you. You have the opportunity to become one with the Divine. Turn inwards for all you seek is waiting patiently inside."

~ Kwali Kumara

MY STORY

I stared at the slightly ajar door of the snake tank where the python should be; a mixture of fear and excitement washed over me.

She's escaped; how clever.

I glanced down at my hands, contemplating my invisible handcuffs and the cage I was in.

Could this be a sign that I, too, can escape from the invisible chains of this horrendous toxic relationship that has me trapped and bound?

I glanced around at the room, which was anything but a home. It was a place I desperately wanted to break free from but didn't know how. Her black and gold silky body was nowhere to be seen. I knew she needed the heat of her vivarium to stay alive, so I began my hunt.

My heart was exploding out of my chest. I didn't even know I was scared of snakes until it was just me and her alone together.

She belonged to my flatmate, who was seldom around. I'd never even been officially introduced to her; now, all of a sudden, she was relying on me to bring her to safety.

As I searched, I contemplated our similar situations, both held in confinement - her in a tank when she should've been in the jungle and me in a toxic relationship and dilapidated house when I should've been enjoying the best years of my life at the tender age of twenty-one.

If she can find freedom, maybe I can too.

I searched for her until the electric meter ran out, cutting my quest short. The lights snapped off like in a horror movie, and as I was plunged into the darkness, I realized looking for a python in pitch black was more than my already-frazzled nervous system could handle.

I prayed she'd find somewhere warm to sleep and I promised I'd find her at first light.

As the sun rose the next day, I woke from a tormented sleep. I dreamt all night about being locked away, unable to move, stuck in hellish places, helpless with no voice. This inquisitive snake that effortlessly pushed open her tank to explore the world outside triggered a process in me, a realization that the door to freedom is always there if we can just have the strength to open it.

I found her almost instantly the next morning.

I'm over here underneath the TV stand in the electricity leads.

Her clever primal instinct had helped her to make a little snuggly camouflaged nest. My heart leaped with excitement that she was still alive and well, even though it was a cold house and she could've been lost forever in its ragged disrepair.

My heart was beating like a hummingbird and I was trembling like a mouse hiding from a predator.

I remember my best friend at secondary school had a strong phobia of snakes; you couldn't even say the S word without her going into a full panic attack. However, I didn't know that I, too, would have any kind of uncomfortable feelings around them until that moment. My third eye spoke to hers.

I'm very honored to meet you and slightly nervous about picking you up, but we need to get you back in your tank so you are warm and safe, will you help me?

Her beautiful, majestic face lifted up, and like royalty, she stared me straight in the eyes.

You have nothing to fear, we are one in La Kesh.

I knew this meant 'I am another yourself' in Mayan.

I knelt in prayer and thanked her for her trust as I caressed her soft, cold body with my warm fingers and felt her energy blend into mine. I cradled her in my arms like a beautiful cosmic baby, a gift from the universe, a glimpse of light in the ocean of darkness that was my current existence.

We bonded, like in the movie Avatar when the Navis let their dreadlocks fuse with their dragon's plumage.

At the time I had no idea how deep and powerful this connection would turn out to be. Little did I know that my flatmate would gift her to me because he could see how strong our bond was.

She gave me the strength to love myself enough to break free from not just that relationship but the next that followed, which was also super unhealthy. Like the power that lives inside each of us, she sat silently sleeping, watching, and waiting for her time to rise. She delivered her sweet medicine of empowerment most gently and humbly. I named her Kundalini. I knew that this was the only appropriate name for such a goddess.

I knew very little about kundalini energy at that time, other than it was depicted as a sleeping snake that resides in the sacred room (sacrum) at the base of the spine.

We had many adventures together, including one incredible night that was purely by accident, but it impacted my life so profoundly. It shaped my destiny and my mission on Earth forever more. I was booked to perform on stage for thousands of people at the Brixton Academy in London. I was a performance artist for some of the coolest dance parties in the city. One night it happened that Kundalini was with me in her basket, I explained to the bouncer that this circumstance was unavoidable and I was worried about leaving her in the car or in a side room where she'd be unsupervised;

"Would you mind if I kept her with me while I do my show? Around my neck is the safest place for her."

He laughed, "No problem."

I couldn't believe how easy he was to convince. He went on to explain,

"Snakes are the only pets allowed in nightclubs so long as they're with their owners. They are deaf so the sound will cause no harm. The rumbling bass line will seem like a herd of elephants."

What an absolute legend he was to give me that permission and understanding so I could dance that night with my beloved serpent sister knowing she wouldn't be under any stress.

We stepped out onto the stage and began to weave our magic together for the sea of adoring ecstatic ravers who suddenly became unusually still. What was a thriving ocean of pulsing, sweaty humans was now a collection of wide-eyed, awestruck, mesmerized creatures with their mouths wide open.

I knew my act was hot, but this was a reaction I never had before. I turned around and looked above the DJ booth only to see that the visuals crew had zoomed their cameras onto Kundalini around my neck; I'd been happily upstaged by my beautiful serpent.

She was live on the massive screen, close up, completely hypnotizing everyone with her presence. Such immense power and a total command of energy from one seemingly humble being. It was then I knew the healing power of the serpent was stronger than anything I had ever encountered before.

After this revelation, I continued to perform with my beloved, and we choreographed our performance in a way that expressed the beauty and grace of her spirit and not the darkness traditionally associated with her kind.

She won the hearts of so many admirers, just like she had won mine that day we were both trapped together.

Now, not only was she free, but she was a famous performance artist in her own right, a healing snake that had adoring fans of her own. Dancing with me in some of the most awesome raves, she found her way to the hot, sweaty, aquatic rainforest conditions she so craved. She had made her way to an urban jungle with warm, sweaty trees in the form of euphoric dancers.

She became so famous that when she ascended in a dramatic accident, someone heard about my tragic loss and was so moved by the tale of our friendship that they gifted me their snake.

I was working in Camden when a lovely lady bought me their Python in a basket, she was the image of Kundalini. I always said that if I was meant to keep a serpent in captivity, I would never buy one, I'd only ever rescue one or accept one as a gift in the same way Kundalini was bestowed to me.

It was as if the Universe heard my prayer, blessing me with an almost identical python whom I still have to this day. She is my oldest snake. I named her Kukulkan, which means plumed serpent in Mayan.

This is how my journey of rescuing snakes began. I now have thirty-three, all bought to me over the last two decades. The most magical part of this is that when Kundalini passed, I was so moved and deeply affected I decided to honor her life by taking up Kundalini Yoga. It became my commitment to her and the time we shared. I was so inspired by the teachings that I trained for over seven years to become a teacher of this incredible technology. My pet snake brought to me my path and my dharma.

I now support people to transform, as I share the serpent teachings with them. I became so passionate my Guru mentored me to birth my own healing modality incorporating live serpents into the technology of kundalini yoga. It's an extremely powerful process of facing your fears in a calm and sacred way. I have yet to fail to get anyone over their fear of snakes, all it takes is enough boldness and bravery to meet me on the yoga mat. Once they trust me they are halfway to freedom from fear, not only do they meet and meditate with the snakes to understand their wisdom, but they also gain a deeper understanding of their own internal life-force energy system.

Serpents are the living, breathing avatars of the yogic teachings. Lord Shiva, the supreme yogi, was always depicted with live snakes as were all of the great gods and goddesses of ancient religions. The Mayans, the Dragon Priests of the Orient, Egyptians, and Hindu Deities all held snakes in high esteem, particularly the plumed serpent, which is a predominant symbol of enlightenment throughout all sacred spiritual cultures.

We have so much to learn from these beautiful mystical creatures. They continue to be my greatest teachers as I've offered myself in service to helping 'give them back their wings.' Once upon a time, they were dragons and their wings were slayed and they fell to Earth.

The serpent is traditionally the symbol of Mother Earth. It's the closest creature to Gaia and her ley lines reflect their form. Great Spirit is naturally associated with wings, representing the heavenly angelic realms. The caduceus, one of the oldest medicine symbols on the planet, is a plumed serpent—a staff of light with two serpents dancing around the central pillar with wings opening at the crown.

This is a literal representation of the kundalini life force energy that resides in every one of us, that can be awakened in this lifetime no matter who you are, so long as you commit to the practice that encourages the energy to make its ascent and open in your crown to achieve a full state of realization in a human body.

It's in every one of us, and it's our birthright, I'm blessed to be able to offer the transmission of these serpent's teachings in this lifetime.

Together, we stand in harmony with our great Mother Earth and almighty Father Sky as we, their sacred children, follow the path of light to create a haven of harmony where we do what needs to be done for the greater good of all.

THE TOOL

I would like to share a potent ancient tool for transformation, a kundalini practice to combat fear:

Release and Renew Through Tattva Yoga (yoga of mudras)

In our lineage, it's traditional to open the space with these sacred mantras. They connect us to our inner teacher, our ancestors, and all the Gurus and guides who have gone before us whom we call 'The Golden Chain.'

We create a safe container, a protective sound current that surrounds our aura while we're meditating. They're not compulsory but strongly advised to get the best medicine from the practice.

Take some deep breaths and center yourself.

Place your hands in a prayer pose and rest the knuckles of your thumbs against your sternum point.

Inhale reaching the crown of the head up to the heavens. Exhale—feel your roots connecting down from your tailbone into Mother Earth.

Inhale, feel your aura expand, exhale, feel yourself land.

Set your intention for your practice by vibrating it mentally through your body in a positive affirmation. You may also wish to offer some of the sweetness of your meditation to a being in the spirit of seva (selfless service). This could be a friend who might need some extra energy at this time or a deity that you align with.

When we perform a sacred act for more than ourselves, it amplifies its medicine and spreads beautiful vibrations out to the world wherever it is needed at the time.

You are ready to begin, take a deep breath, and chant the two mantras below three times each.

I have included the translation for your reference but you will chant only in Gurmukhi (the ancient sacred language of the Sikhs.)

ONG NAMO GURU DEV NAMO (three times)

"I bow to the Infinite Creative Consciousness. I bow to the Divine Wisdom, the teacher within and without."

AAD GURAY NAMEH, JUGAAD GURAY NAMEH, SAAT GURAY NAMEH, SIRI GURU DEVAY NAMEH (three times)

(I bow to the primal wisdom. I bow to the wisdom through the ages. I bow to the true Wisdom. I bow to the great unseen wisdom.)

Sit cross-legged, half-lotus, or full-lotus. Use cushions under your knees to make you feel comfortable. If you are not relaxed on the floor, a chair is fine. The most important thing is that your spine is straight, and your head sits on the sternal notch.

The following meditation is thirteen minutes long, but it can be shortened, to begin with, and you can build it up in time.

Start with your hands in Kapitthaka Mudra.

In English this is called the Fearless Mudra, it turns the direction of the mind and removes doubt and fear; it is performed exactly as the famous hippy peace sign of the seventies.

Hold both hands out slightly to the side of your body, facing forward, with your elbows tucked into your waist, and then begin opening and closing your fingers as if they were scissors. Your index finger connects to the planet Jupiter (wisdom), and your middle finger is connected to Saturn (emotion). It will feel very irritating and slightly annoying, but just keep doing it; you're clearing your karma and all the stored emotions, fears, and phobias from your subconscious.

The more you detest it, the more it's working! Keep going for eleven minutes.

Breathe in through the nose, and out through the nose, and no matter what your mind says or does to try and get you to stop, DO NOT! Just keep going; you're healing yourself on a deep cellular level.

Your eyes remain closed throughout and the focus is on your third eye (Ajna chakra) in the center of your forehead.

Once your timer hits eleven minutes, continue with the moving mudra, but make an O shape with your mouth as if you were sucking through a straw and breathe in and out of your mouth as you continue the snipping mudra.

Imagine you're cutting away all the negativity from your life, all the sorrow, the pain, the trauma, the fear, everything that no longer serves you.

Snip, snip, snip, let the breath become as powerful as it needs to be to blow not just your troubles away but those of your ancestors who have gone before you. You're cleaning seven generations of karma both before and after your existence.

Excellent work!

The movement is continued for two-and-a-half additional minutes, thirteen and a half altogether. To finish, take a big breath in and hold it as you make the body as strong as steel, and then:

Repeat three times.

The last exhale should be the most powerful as you empty yourself completely. Resume regular breathing and meditate in silence absorbing and processing the medicine of the meditation.

When you feel ready, begin rubbing your palms together starting at the crown of the head and working your way down to the base, grounding yourself to Mother Earth and back into your heart where we remain in unconditional love, gratitude, service, and grace.

Let your hands rest in a prayer pose once again.

To end we chant SAT NAM three times.

Sat means truth, and *Nam* means name; 'Truth is our vibration/name.' The *sat* is very long, and the *nam* is very short, symbolizing a long life with a short death.

Make any final prayers for peace and healing, and then bow your head in reverence to give thanks for your beautiful existence.

To get the best results from this meditation, practice it every day for forty consecutive days to seal its magic into your cells. If you miss a day, go back to the beginning; that way, you will be fully committed, and you'll make sure you get the job done.

Good luck, and please reach out for more information, spiritual guidance, and teachings. I have a huge archive of recordings, including classes, meditations, and ceremonies for you to enjoy in my Kundalini Temple of Teachings.

https://www.kundalinitemple.com/

https://www.elementalhealingtemple.com/

Kwali Kumara is a magnetic, uplifting, and inspiring international Kundalini Yoga and meditation teacher, spiritual guide, serpent healer, sacred ceremonialist, mantra artist, Starchild yoga teacher, NLP coach, Yin Yoga instructor, Shamanic Energy healer, Galactic Gong Goddess, Egyptian Sekhem and Sacred Sound practitioner.

Kwali qualified as a Kundalini instructor in 2008. She has completed all the advanced teaching modules and is a registered member of KYTA.

Kwali has a very experiential background in shamanism, having worked with some incredible guides, mentors, and medicine carriers. She walked the shamanic road for many years before stepping onto the yogic path during her Saturn returns.

She is the pioneer of 'Serpent Healing,' a holistic therapy created to help students overcome their phobias, release trauma, and ignite their personal power in a unique and exciting way. This transformational work inspires a more insightful understanding of one's own life-force energy and activates a stronger relationship to it. It enhances a sacred and mystical connection to Great Spirit and Mother Earth while helping students gain a deeper, more profound understanding of snake medicine and kundalini energy.

Kwali is an accomplished multiple Galactic Gong player with over a decade of experience in sacred sound ceremonies. She is also a recording artist and has released five albums with her prolific producer, Pete Ardron.

Kwali is the host and curator of the 'Ceremony Space' for the legendary 'Mind Body Spirit' festivals in London and Birmingham. She has been co-creating with them for eight years and is one of their treasured resident presenters and practitioners.

This year she is launching her own 'Elemental Temple Festival' in Oxfordshire, which is a fundraiser for her 'Plumed Serpent Sanctuary' and 'The Rainforest Trust.'

Kwali lives a rural life in Cambridgeshire with her partner, son, daughter, three cats, her little dog, and beloved rescued snakes.

Connect with Kwali at:

https://www.kundalinitemple.com/

https://www.elementalhealingtemple.com/

CHAPTER 15

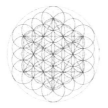

THE VIOLET RAINBOW

TRANSFORMATIONAL ENERGY FOR HEALING

Joan Osborne

MY STORY

"You can't be a healer. You still need to be healed yourself."

This was the curt response when I asked to join a local spiritualist church healing group years ago.

This hit me hard and highlighted my biggest challenge—to believe in myself and have the confidence to become a healer and teacher. To trust the guidance I receive is not just imagination; to know I have a role to play, and part of that is helping others to receive the healing they need and begin to believe in their worth too.

However, the Beloved (the beings who guide and inspire me) were full of encouragement.

Listen to your own heart and intuition. Others cannot decide who or what you are. They cannot see you as we do. You can be the healer you want to be—and more!

I realized we can be healers and channel that beautiful energy while still receiving healing for ourselves. Indeed, I believe we cannot be fully healed on **all** levels while in the physical world. If that were so, we wouldn't be here!

Devoting time to widening and honing my skills, I relied on the Beloved to show me the way. Under their guidance, I held various workshops focusing on bringing healing on many levels and using my voice to sing light language tonings.

One workshop dealt with the adverse cord attachments between people. Years before, I experienced a healing form where the cord was severed with golden scissors. Without really knowing why, I didn't feel comfortable with the process. My Beloved now made it clear this was not the way—at least for me!

They showed me that unconditional love and forgiveness needed to be fully received to bathe and dissolve the root within. That loving energy was then allowed to flow into and along the cord until it reached the second root so that it, too, was dissolved and cleansed. A true transformation!

Then came the year I was diagnosed with cancer—a time of both challenge and huge blessing!

Early in the year, I was meditating and suddenly felt the presence of Archangel Azrael.

It is time, he said.

I felt a bit nervous because Azrael, the Archangel of Life and Death, is portrayed as rather stern, but I held myself ready for whatever was to come.

At this stage, I'd like to explain that most transmissions of knowledge I've received in recent years have been through strong inflows of energy rather than actual dialogue. In short, the energy seems to embed itself within me.

Azrael's intent was clear as he touched me with a little of the platinum ray energy. My workshops each needed to evolve further and be given as a series to enable platinum ray healing to come forward into these dimensions.

Both excited and humbled by this, I began to plan out the months ahead as the process of many healing aspects now took on a much deeper and more powerful vibrancy under Azrael's inspiration.

Having completed the initial stages by April 2015, I was diagnosed with breast cancer and needed surgery to remove a small tumor, which proved to be malignant. Fortunately, chemotherapy was deemed unnecessary, but I had several weeks of intense radiotherapy.

Throughout all, I knew the Beloveds were with me and this was proved beyond doubt when, during one prolonged wait for treatment, they guided me to write of the creation of soul seeds and souls. Combined with wonderful imagery, the information was given over many minutes, part of which was:

Radiating from Source multitudinous streams and spirals of energetic matter. Matter made up of sparks of Light, each a galaxy within itself and the potential to expand. These are soul seeds – a direct emanation of Divine Force carrying the inspiration of creation..... From the soul seed is born the 'Golden I Am Presence' which in turn creates the soul....

Once my course of treatment was completed, I continued the series until, in the penultimate workshop, Archangel Azrael gave us the blessing of knowing the platinum portal opened enough to allow the energy to begin to flow into our reality, to bring another dimension to healing work.

Azrael then inspired the creation of The Violet Rainbow—a merging of the Violet Flame and Melchizedek's Healing Rainbow, imbued with the influence of the platinum ray.

This brought in deeper levels of healing to do with the inner realms of our being, those hidden layers where we hold so much suppressed fear, grief, guilt, and more, including ancestral and karmic issues.

I've seen people cry with relief when freed of an old inhibiting belief pattern, or feel a greater sense of self-worth. One beautiful lady was finally able to open up and know that she, too, deserved to be loved!

The Violet Rainbow is constantly evolving, and each time I offer the energy to clients or in workshops, I feel the changing intensity of the healing potential. Combined with my light language tones, there are moments it seems to radiate a new unlimited power. Indeed, during one workshop meditation, it felt as if we were standing on the edge of time looking into Infinity. We thought we had been there for hours, but the clock registered only five minutes!

There is one standard I adopted and which I recommend—the use of a fail-safe like "**for the Highest good**" or "**In accord with Divine will and Highest good**"—whichever feels most natural. I always give this intent and feel it's especially vital when sending absent healing (where you have not first received permission) to others.

I also believe we cannot decide how healing will work. Not being physically healed may be what's needed, however harsh that may seem. Rather the healing focus is to resolve deeply hidden or unacknowledged fears and traumas.

Some feel it isn't necessary to set up protection or use a fail-safe when giving healing, but I believe it's a wise precaution as none of us knows exactly what's needed. Also, we may carry an unconscious bias about how the healing should work, particularly if there's an element of emotional involvement. But the soul knows exactly what is needed and why.

Honoring that choice is as natural as breathing for me.

THE TOOL

Aligning to and receiving The Violet Rainbow needs intent and willingness. As always, the more you use it, the easier it becomes.

This attunement connects you to the energy so that you can use it for yourself as needed.

Recordings of the attunement and healing exercises can be made available!

First, set your space as usual.

MEDITATION AND ATTUNEMENT TO THE VIOLET RAINBOW:

Give time to go through the process in a steady and measured way.

- Ensure you're seated comfortably, with your feet on the floor, and hands rested in a comfortable position.
- Take a deep breath in—as deep as you can without strain. Then let the breath out and relax! Close your eyes, allowing the chair to take your full weight. Take another deep breath and, as you breathe out, relax even more.
- Give the intent you are open to receive, to be blessed with the energy of the Violet Rainbow as is right and good for you.
- All around you are specks of multi-colored light. Breathe them in and then breathe out with a sigh, relaxing even more. Repeat this twice more so that these glowing specks of light fill your body with their

brilliance. Feel the rainbow light within you, beginning to expand your awareness, expanding your ability to receive.

- Now imagine or become aware of a doorway opening up before you, a doorway opening wide in welcome. A gentle, loving energy flows out to embrace you, drawing you to the threshold. Here, you are held, supported, and loved. Rest in that support and love. Feel it hold you firmly balanced and steady.

Pause for a moment.

- Slowly you become aware of two magnificent beings glowing with radiant light standing on either side of you. These are the Archangels Melchizedek and Azrael. On either side of Melchizedek and Azrael stand more angelic beings and masters, each holding one of the many vibrational streams of energy that is part of the two rays—the Violet and the Rainbow. They seem to burn brighter and brighter until their energies unite and merge. The rainbow energy of Melchizedek unites with the layers of platinum violet energy of Azrael.

- Let yourself be bathed in this kaleidoscope of color and bright energy for a moment and take a slow, deep breath.

- As you breathe in, more beings come to stand behind you, including two angelic beings, the sacred sisters—Azrael's emissaries. They stand gently radiating their energy towards you.

- Breathe in that loving energy—their strength and support are with you.

- Breathe again. Let the energy flow through your being until you're filled with sacred Light.

Pause

- The energy holds you gently as ripples stir the ethers far away. It's as if veils of illusion are parting to allow a great dragon to flow towards you. This great dragon is black as the darkest night but glows within with the myriad colors of the Divine rainbow. He comes closer and closer until he is immediately in front of you, and you feel his breath bathing you in a gentle and powerful glow.

- As he joins with the archangels and other beings, the Violet Rainbow takes on a new dimension, as if it's being reborn. It throbs with new power and transformational force.

Breathe and allow.

- This powerful force now gently and slowly begins to flow towards you, first just touching, then enfolding and wrapping you around, holding you in a whirling stream of multi-colored energy, supporting you, keeping you steady.

- The dragon's breath gains strength and power, blowing through you like a strong wind, dragging up many strands of fear and doubt, transforming them with love. He is preparing the way so you may receive more fully.

Pause

- The Violet Rainbow energy now flows all around. Breathe it in. Allow it to flow through your whole body. Imagine it going through your body from the top of your head to the soles of your feet. Feel or imagine this energy pouring into you, not just on the breath but through your skin and every part of you, holding you gently but strongly. Let the energy fill your being, then allow it to flow into your life. No need to focus on details; just let it flow.

- Give your permission—your intent—that it will bring needed transformation and healing to your life, to the here and now, to the past and all that has been, to the future and all that is to be. No need to focus on specific aspects; just let it flow with the intent this healing will bring in what is needed for your own highest good.

- Breathe and allow the energy to flow down through your body into the Earth beneath, to give to the planet some of the energy that has been gifted to you.

Pause

- The energy builds all around you, sparkling and sparking with power and light, holding you safe in an orb of transformational healing love.

- Sit with this energy for a while, allowing it to flow into and through you.

Pause. Allow about two to five minutes only at this stage as it is a very powerful energy.

- Now gently take a breath, then another. As you do so, Azrael and Melchizedek place a blessing into your heart and higher brow chakras to seal the energy within. The dragon circles around you once more and then glides back into his own realm.

- The other beings gently withdraw also, but the two magnificent archangels stand on each side of you, holding you in a cocoon of energy to help steady the force within; to give your energy field the strength it needs to absorb this new potential.

- Breathe and allow. You need these moments to absorb the steadying influence and blessing of these two mighty beings for they love YOU.

- *Pause for a few moments.*

- Now take another breath and allow any images or sensations to slowly fade as the Violet Rainbow energy flows back into the portal from which it came, knowing that the blessing set within you holds the seed of this amazing energy so it's available to you at any time. Give thanks to the archangels Azrael and Melchizedek, the sacred sisters, the Violet Rainbow dragon, and all those wonderful beings who came forward with such great love to bring you this beautiful energy. Remember to include your guardians and guides who have stayed close by.

- Breathe in deeply and allow your awareness to focus steadily back into your physical body.

- Take another deep breath, and as you breathe out, breathe down to your feet. Keep breathing in and breathing down, bringing your awareness back into the present time and place. Become aware of the weight of your body upon the seat, your feet upon the floor. Wiggle your fingers and toes to help bring you fully back into the present time and place. When you are ready, open your eyes.

Take time with grounding; this is a powerful energy.

HEALING YOURSELF

This is a focused way of receiving the Violet Rainbow healing energy, although do please use it with respect both for its power and for yourself. As always, give the intent that all be in accord with your own highest good.

You may wonder why this particular method is suggested. Many of us have an unconscious reluctance to accept healing for ourselves, finding it easier to send healing to others. Using a mirror image helps overcome this. It becomes easier to receive healing, and the energy seems to intensify. However, you may find another way that feels more comfortable for you.

Exercise:

- Ensure you're seated comfortably, with your feet on the floor, and close your eyes. Breathe in as deep as you can without strain, then let it go on a gentle sigh and relax.

- Take another breath in, letting it gently go and relaxing even more. Now breathe naturally.

- Begin to become aware of the Violet Rainbow portal opening up close behind you; streams of energy full of color and vibrancy gently reach into your heart, opening it up more and more. The Violet Rainbow dragon takes up position (to your right, left, or behind as is right for you) and begins to breathe gently into and through you; opening you up even more to the transformational healing power of the energy; bringing another vibrant level to it all.

Pause for a moment.

- As your heart fills and overflows, allow the energy to begin to flow out into the space before you like a beam of beautiful light.

- Allow this beam to form an orb of light before you.

- Now imagine you're being held within that orb. In essence, a mirror image of you is facing you.

- Take a breath, allowing the energy of the Violet Rainbow to begin to flow from the mirror image in that orb directly to you so that it's beaming out from your heart to the mirror image and then reflecting directly back into yourself. Breathe it in; let it fill you up. Just allow it to do what it needs to do for **you!**

Pause for a minute or so.

- The Violet Rainbow dragon now gently takes hold of the orb, giving even more of his radiance to the healing energy as it moves backward and forward. It is then as if he is both before and behind you, and he opens his heart fire so that its glow enfolds both you and your mirror image. Breathe it in.

- Now take a deep breath and allow that mirror image to gently fade as the energy of the orb is absorbed back into yourself.

- As the dragon withdraws his vibrancy let the energy of the Violet Rainbow flow gently and steadily back into its own portal.

- The dragon breathes over you one last time then returns to his own realm.

- Breathe again and let the portal gently close.

- Give thanks to Azrael, Melchizedek, the Violet Rainbow dragon, and all the wonderful beings who aided in this healing.

- Now, take several deep breaths, bringing yourself back into the moment, grounding, and centering as strongly as you can.

Again, take time and care to be grounded and steady.

The mirror image may send light and/or color like a laser beam to certain parts of your body to focus healing energy exactly where needed. The dragon may also focus energy on specific areas. It will always be as is right for you in the moment.

A note of caution: Some people try to deal with everything at once! Take your time; the key is safe and steady!

Joan Osborne is a healer, teacher, and Sister of Dragons, with over 30 years of experience on the path and having trained in various healing modalities, including becoming a Reiki Master and teacher (Usui tradition).

With strong connections to other dimensions, her beliefs are based on Universal Love and the inner potential of all. Working with many light beings (archangels, angels, dragons, and more), she is honored to be guided by their wisdom and inspiration, including channeling the transmission of energy via focused intent and light language tonings/song.

It has become natural for Joan to refer to these many beings as 'The Beloved' as she knows their love is always with her.

When she began her journey, the guidance given was more verbal, as she needed that method of clear instruction. However, in recent years, it has become more of a process of osmosis as she is bathed in the energy she is being asked to work with. Nevertheless, the Beloveds do make cogent observations and comments to be passed on or to bring in elements of laughter and joy.

Joan has offered workshops and personal healing sessions within the UK for over 20 years, being a regular workshop facilitator at The College of Psychic Studies. In addition, she offers remote healing sessions both nationally and internationally.

Her constantly evolving workshops are each linked to the transformational healing of those deeper layers where so many fears, traumas, and inhibiting belief patterns are held.

She is the founder of several workshops, including Transforming Ties that Bind, The Violet Rainbow, and The Power of Compassion.

Although in her senior years, Joan remains active in all her healing work and feels truly blessed to see the positive effects many enjoy.

Connect with Joan:

Website: www.healing-vibrations.com

CHAPTER 16

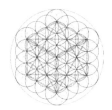

THE WEB OF WOMBS ACTIVATION

REUNITE AS THE MAGDALENES TO WEAVE THE NEW EARTH

Stefanie Kernler

MY STORY

It has taken me almost 40 years to arrive in my body entirely. For a big part of my life, it felt like it took an effort to be me.

There was a time I couldn't connect with myself, when my needs were a weird mystery. I was a dormant soul, asleep in my body.

This is an Instagram post I wrote about four years ago.

I struggled a lot in the past days and weeks. I felt numb towards what served me. I felt constantly tired. Unmotivated. I knew what it would have taken to feel better, but I couldn't change it.

There is this strange feeling deep inside me. It was much stronger when I was younger (and got much better when I stopped taking the pill at 28 years old), but it is still there.

When I am so tired I can barely keep my eyes open, I ignore my body telling me I need sleep (urgently) and push myself to stay awake (for no good reason).

Sometimes, I feel like jumping in the crystal clear mountain river down the road, and yet I find excuses not to do it, even though my whole body is screaming for the refreshing excitement.

Sometimes, my body hurts from carrying around a toddler all day. And yet, I don't stretch or take a bath, although I know it's what my body longs for.

I was doing my best and realized it wasn't enough. And as a mother, this was mirrored back at me by my child 24/7. There was no hiding any longer.

I watched my partner play with our little daughter for ages and realized I couldn't do the same. After a short while, I always needed to go away to "fix" something—do the dishes, check the phone, get a drink, go to the bathroom, etc. while he played with her for hours.

While the sun ignited our room in the most beautiful light, sadness built within me.

I realized I could only connect to her as much as I could connect to myself. I longed for more.

How can I stop cheating about my future with my past?

How can I live a deeply nourishing and fulfilling life?

Can I give more to my daughter?

Can I ask more of motherhood?

I was done with playing small.

"I will keep you posted on how it goes" was the sentence I ended my Instagram post with. So, in a way, this story is my update—my way to keep you posted.

The birth of our daughter was my spiritual awakening at the age of 36.

To bring her Earth-side gifted me with a sacred connection to my womb, the Divine, to the power of shakti and kundalini, and the essence of my soul.

To give birth to this beautiful light angel forever changed me and my perception of life.

At the same time, I painfully realized something blocked my connection to self-love and the love I could give to her and others.

So here we are on the kitchen floor. The sweetest nine-month-old baby girl looks at her mother, who cannot connect with her deeply and be present because she never learned how to connect and be present with herself. Her mother cannot give her unconditional love because she never felt unconditional love for herself (which is a huge topic in my mother line).

My inner journey to find profound connection and love within myself started. I was guided on a journey to awaken my heart and womb consciousness.

Along the way, I had a few profound realizations:

My curiosity about the spiritual dimensions of conception, pregnancy, birth, and motherhood made me understand how my earliest imprints, from pre-conception to early childhood, shaped me for life.

I discovered I was never truly welcomed into this world.

Everything makes so much sense. Now I understand why it always takes an effort to be seen, heard, accepted, and loved!

I was induced and born with a suction cup. I was never given the time to arrive in the time of my soul.

This is why I'm always late and do things at the last minute. I feel rushed to be on time and do not trust my inner knowing and guidance, but I seem to copy the knowing and guidance of others.

All of this was mirrored back at me in my own story and the long womb history of my mother-line with cancer and blocked energies, ending up in many diseases.

I realized I was energetically blocked from conceiving a baby the same way I was blocked from enjoying life to the fullest.

Wait, is there a link between how we perceive life and our earliest imprints of life?

Is there a link between our womb and how we perceive or create our reality?

These questions aren't just for me to ponder. They're for all women to explore together, to deepen our understanding of ourselves, and why so many of us struggle to conceive and how it relates to our connection within and the world around us.

I gave birth to three girls in this lifetime, and each of these birth experiences brought healing to my own story once I integrated their sacred teachings.

Every single one of my births offered me a doorway to my spiritual power and a new level of consciousness. And, of course, all this links back to my own soul's path; it's all interwoven.

This story is not just about me. It's about all of us and the power we hold within ourselves to transform and grow from maiden to mother to maga to crone, from isolation to freedom, from functioning to thriving, alchemizing and claiming.

Our stories and wombs are interwoven.

Here is my story and the sacred teachings I was gifted with in the birth portal:

1. Listen within and speak your truth.

2. Stop playing small and embody a radiant womb.

3. Let go, trust, and become one with the web of life.

My first birth was an abortion, and it took me years to understand and integrate the teachings and thrive as a mother and woman.

Step by step, layer by layer, I looked for guidance from all three births and connected the dots.

I began to work on my mindset and spiritual evolution. I needed to recognize and alchemize the emotional and energetic blocks that were holding me back before I gained access to certain frequencies of the spirit baby realm, and was guided to work with the Divine Mother and the Magdalene energies within the web of wombs.

My conceptions, pregnancies, births, breastfeeding and postpartum experiences taught me who I am and what soul path I have chosen in this lifetime.

Step by step, I was breaking free and becoming a Mother of the New Earth.

After 40 years, I fully arrived in my body through the womb work and spiritual development I claimed as a mother.

When I was first introduced to Mary Magdalene in a guided meditation, it instantly hit me.

I am her.

I understood she was a part of me, and she did not exist outside of me. She exists within all of us.

I made space to meet her in silence.

I understood stop playing small is not only about me and the women on earth holding back, but about me and the women on earth connecting, weaving and co-creating.

From that moment on, everything changed.

Magically, powerful projects came into my life. Magically, others sensed the energy of Mary Magdalene within me.

I feel seen. We recognize each other.

Through this realization, new timelines were formed and the guidance from within was loud and clear.

I realized we are many. I realized our time is now.

With tears in my eyes and a heart full of love, I saw the web of wombs forming. I was called to weave in the web of wombs with other women, knowing we have been prepared for this co-creation throughout many lifetimes.

Spirit called me to let go of anything I did up until now and create space for the new.

Spirit called us to co-create.

Spirit guided us to connect and step into our power.

A rush of pure ecstasy ran through my body. It was time to reunite as the Magdalenes.

A magical doorway opened for me and all women to step into our fullest soul expression and embody our leadership for the new.

I am here to hold and witness women in their power when they claim back their awakened wombs and co-create a life filled with love, peace, abundance, prosperity, and joy for us and our children.

It was a journey of six years where spirit took me to Australia, Bali, Mexico, and the UK to reclaim and remember.

It was a journey that nearly forced a divorce (we aren't even married), as my partner was afraid I'd gone mad many times along the way.

It was a journey where I came to see the Goddess within myself and all women.

It was a journey where spirit babies started to guide their mothers from all over the world to find me, to co-create and weave magic together.

It was a journey of deep fulfillment (and sometimes of maximum loneliness and frustration).

It was a journey where, financially, I fed my soul business for many years until I understood what needed to shift for my soul business to feed me.

I was guided by the souls of my daughters and my partner, learning how our soul contracts are closely linked in this lifetime.

It daunted me. Spirit guided me to visit the womb and heart centers of the world to claim, remember, and bring forth the teachings and activations of the web of wombs.

After all these years, everything was falling into place. I couldn't believe it, and yet I felt it all along.

I was coming home in the web of wombs.

For every woman, the journey is different. Yet, in the web of wombs, every single woman frees a sacred part of herself and the collective. We are accompanied by the spirit babies and the children on Earth, by our ancestors and bloodline.

You can descend into the sacred darkness of your womb with a clear intention or enter the hive fully open to soften and receive, to process and integrate, to replenish and regenerate, or to receive guidance and activation.

In the web of wombs, you experience yourself in your fullest soul expression. You don't only understand that all is in you, but you experience it.

In the web of wombs, we're all mirrors and medicine for each other, and every one of us represents millions of women. We feel the womb connection that connects us back to the first mother.

In the web of wombs, we remember through our connection and start to drink from the endless flow of golden nectar. Our wombs start to radiate, and our empty divine female cups start to overflow. We set ourselves free, and we embody a new, vibrant energy.

We don't channel any energy from above or below, but we activate sacred womb codes from within. The web of wombs forms in divine timing, riding the dragon energy just as we signed up for.

The web of wombs is about freedom, love, and peace. These are the foundations for a life in which we embody the Divine Feminine and create the world we want to see for our children and families.

So much is possible when we step into the power of the web of wombs, the creatrix of life. It's a radiant gateway to our mystical power and energy.

In the web of wombs, we have nothing to hide.

In the web of wombs, we are all mothers to each other. Every child is your child (now, let this sink in!).

We are interwoven as the bringers of life, as the creators. And as such, we can co-create a new reality rooted in the power of love, embodying divine feminine wholeness through our awakened wombs.

We were always meant to rise together, weaving magic from the womb connection we hold with each other.

If this speaks to you, I invite you with all my heart and soul to establish a deeper connection to your womb consciousness and to join us in the web of wombs. You are awaited.

THE TOOL

The Guidance:

Know about your earliest imprints and rites of passage and how they shaped you for life.

Step 1: First, I want you to connect with your womb.

Your womb is the energy center of your female energies and affects all aspects of your life: the way you think and feel, your sexual energy, your creativity and spirituality, and how you connect with others and the world. Journal about the following question.

• If your womb could talk, what would it say?

Please do this exercise out in nature, letting Spirit guide you to a place that feels aligned and peaceful.

Give yourself as much time as you need and journal from your heart and womb, pen on paper.

Once you've completed the exercise, read out loud what you wrote. What is revealed to you? Mark some of the keywords and breathe deeply.

Step 2: Journal about how you came into this life.

- What do you know about your conception, pregnancy, birth, and postnatal or breastfeeding experience?

Write down whatever you know, and if you have a chance, talk to your mum about it to find out. Ask specific questions about how she felt instead of just receiving hard facts (natural birth, C-section), etc.

Step 3: Reflect on how you usually manage projects.

This can be anything from planning a birthday party to how you perform at work. Write as much as you want, and take enough time to see what patterns emerge.

- How do you usually start a project? Is it easy for you to generate ideas?
- How do you usually manage projects? Are you very coordinated, all over the place, always doing a million things simultaneously, etc.?
- How do you usually complete projects? On time, earlier, late?
- How do you usually manage your projects once they are completed? Keep things up to date, or lose interest?

Pause here and only read further once you have answered all questions.

So here is the jazz I've learned from Anna Verwaal (From Womb to World) and Jane Hardwicke Collings (School of Shamanic Womancraft). I wish everybody would understand these profound patterns and connections:

Conception is how ideas come to you. It's how you live, how you are creative, and how you birth projects.

Pregnancy is how you bring ideas to life. It's how you turn ideas into reality. How do you approach it?

Birth (first contraction until the placenta is born) is how you finish projects. It's how you finalize your projects.

Your postnatal experience mirrors how you look after everything you create. It's how you take care of your projects.

The better you understand your patterns and imprints, the better you can cope, integrate, and transform them.

Connect with your intuition and womb wisdom

This is simple yet powerful and life-changing:

Your intuition is your inner compass, your inner guidance. I came to understand it's like a muscle you can train with one simple exercise per day.

Ready?

Step 1: Every morning, when you wake up, pause to listen within. Make space for the very first guidance you receive.

- What is my soul longing for today?

It can be simple things like cutting roses in front of your house, stepping outside to feel the sun kissing your face, or having a warm, nourishing drink.

Now, it's essential to make space for whatever guidance you receive and prioritize it in the morning, ideally, first thing. Do not let your kids stop you but be a role model instead and show them our inner guidance matters.

You'll see how your whole day starts to unfold in a completely different way, how your frequency is rising, and how so much guidance flows to you while you do it. I have the feeling the more the universe can trust us with this, the more guidance comes through.

So go on, train that muscle. Attune to your intuition and inner guidance, and be curious about how your day and life unfold.

Step 2: The power of your blood codes

One essential step to awakening your womb is honoring the cycles, your ancestors, and your bloodline.

For me, Mary Magdalene's energy is the alchemy of womb consciousness, sexual energy and the blood codes we hold within. Connecting with this energy opens a whole new universe to the Divine Feminine energies we came here to master, and it reminds us about the connection that is forgotten.

- Collect your blood in a glass jar and hold it against the sun.
- Observe the richness, the magical color (it reminds me of the codes of Mary Magdalene), and the life pulsating within. This act became a ceremony for me of the ancient wisdom and connection encoded in my blood.

- Let your intuition guide you to a place in nature where the Earth's heartbeat resonates with your own. Sit in silence, taking in Mother Earth's whispers.

- Give your blood back to Mother Earth. Pour it into the water or onto the soil, returning to the source from where it once came, and open yourself to receive. See how your blood dissolves with the water or sinks into the soil, returning home and becoming one.

I always felt a sacred bond was forged in that moment—a symbiotic connection between woman and Earth, blood and water, blood and soil, blood and bone, blood and the codes of Mother Earth.

May it support you in your womb awakening and activation. May it help you find the power of creation and the ancestral wisdom in your blood. It's within the codes of our blood that we reclaim our sovereignty, our connection to the divine feminine, and our place in the cosmic tapestry of forming a new Earth. It's within our blood we return to our radiant wombs and even when our bleeding ceases, the journey deepens: we dance with the moon, life, and earth cycles, and are initiated to weave the future for all grandchildren.

Powerful soul, I want to hear from you

How is our story interwoven? How can I serve you?

Together we raise the frequency on Earth.

Together we co-create the new.

Together we claim back our power.

Together we weave.

Sat Nam

Stefanie Kernler is a mother of three daughters, a Magdalene Womb Alchemist, Spirit Baby Guide, Divine Conception and Soul Birth Priestess, Light Weaver, Moon Mother, and Yoga teacher. A pioneer in the realm of the awakened feminine, she serves as an alchemist for the energies of the New Earth.

Stefanie is the founder of "Stop Playing Small" and works with women worldwide from pre-conception to pregnancy, birth, and into motherhood and beyond. It's often the spirit babies directing their mothers from all over the world to seek her wisdom and support in guiding souls from universe to womb to world. In the past 15 years, she has guided over 500 souls and inspired thousands worldwide to co-create and weave magic together.

She now brings her soul's work of reuniting women as the Magdalenes, facilitating powerful womb co-creations that infuse Mother Earth with a new frequency and that open new light channels for spirit babies to come Earth-side.

Connect with Stefanie and experience the magic of the web of wombs yourself.

linktr.ee/stopplayingsmall

https://stop-playing-small.com

CHAPTER 17

ANGELIC VORTEX HEALING

WORKING WITH THE ANGELS FOR CLARITY IN YOUR LIFE

Caroline Mary

MY STORY

God, where are the healers in this place?

I sat watching the patients in the sparsely decorated psychiatric ward, wondering if I was tripping. I check myself.

No, not tripping or dreaming. Worst nightmare come true!

Some kind of soul challenge, perhaps?

It feels ironic being here, having once studied the philosophy of mental health and decided the people stuck in these places were the persecuted witches of the modern day, and the doctors their persecutors.

Now I'm witnessing it firsthand!

Real funny Spirit, real funny. I look to the ceiling as I silently curse my guides.

My fellow patients shuffle around in their dressing gowns and slippers, moving from plastic-covered armchairs in the smoke-stained lounge to the hard plastic chairs in the communal dining room. They're carrying flimsy cups of drinks from the machine in one hand and clutching their fags in the other.

God, I've got to get out of this place. They think I'm crazy, but this place is making me crazy!

Where are the people who can really help these folks?

Where are the healers? Where are the psychics?

Nurses look on, taking notes behind the reinforced windows of the medical station, and we're left to amuse ourselves.

I spend my time praying with some patients, sitting on the faded wooden bench outside the front door. Littered with dog-ends, it's the favorite sun spot when you're let out for a short break.

With other patients, I sensed what was happening for them, assuring them they weren't imagining the spirits around them or the emotions running through their system. Some patients became friends as we spent time sharing thoughts about past lives, musing how we knew each other in bygone eras.

These are my people, yet we're being locked up! It's like a prison!

Throughout my days, I'd shiver as dense energies swirled around me and somehow knew to clear them through the ceiling and the floor, calling out silently: *I'm with God, I'm with God, I'm with God.* Other times I sensed spirits coming and going, speaking with them or ushering them away if they felt unhelpful.

The experience was amazing yet exhausting. I was in a hospital with no healing for me, and I just wanted to help the people where the staff couldn't meet their spiritual needs. It was a steep learning curve, for which I was grateful, yet I felt alone and just wanted to go home.

Luckily, phone calls are allowed in this ward, and on a call with an understanding friend, she handed the phone over to her mother. "Caroline, you're so sensitive and need to look after your energy," she encouraged me. "Put a bubble of white light around you, and it'll help you feel clearer."

It was the first energy training I received in my life. And it worked!

I felt calm and relaxed, no longer in fight or flight and pushing against the ridiculous rules. I started to unplug from the chaos and realized I had to play the game to get out.

Soon, this second experience of being locked up started to feel a whole lot easier, and I employed a barrister. He worked his magic in a tribunal, and I was released to go home.

For weeks before being admitted, I experienced a kundalini awakening, and my psychic senses came online. *Big time.* I had streams of information coming through my mind and started to sense and talk to spirits around me.

Family members and friends worried because I was so different from the Caroline they'd known all their lives. I must have seemed strange to them because their psychic senses had yet to open, and nothing I said made any sense to them.

But for me, my soul was coming alive. I was coming home.

After the experience in the hospital, I learned to dumb down my experiences and stop sharing with people, fearing they'd think I was "having an episode" again, thanks to the stigma of the mental health system. I carried with me the fear of getting locked up again and learned to toe the line. I got a new job and got on with life the best I could.

Years later, while traveling through Portugal, I finally committed to my spiritual path during a shamanic ceremony. I cut my beloved dreadlocks and started giving my belongings away as memories came flooding back of speaking to spirits and receiving spiritual knowledge. It was a watershed moment that changed my life.

Despite the peace this commitment brought me, coming back to the UK after the trip was challenging. I was committed to the path, yet where was I headed?

What will I do?

The spiritual commitment led me to separate from my partner. I had to be free to go with my soul's flow. I landed in a new city, staying with an old friend, my remaining things cluttered around me in my room. My now-ex-partner drove off with the camper we shared as home for the last year and a half.

Shit! What am I going to do now?

Remembering something guided me this far, I prayed and came across a local shamanic practitioner. The meeting changed the course of my life.

"I can see the feet of a light being, and now his torso, and now his wings! Oh, it's Archangel Michael!" Anna exclaims. The shamanic practitioner I found relays the vision she's having as she calls in a guide for me in my time of transition.

I can see her vision too, exactly as she's describing it.

Somehow, I knew it was Archangel Michael before she said it. If I'm seeing what she's seeing, am I psychic too?

We felt the energy of this mighty being fill the room as she came back from the journey, and we spoke about why he came forward: to guide me on my path of purpose.

The energy of Archangel Michael stayed with me for weeks, though the next time I saw him was while attending a healing group. Gathering together with new friends, we're standing together, hands touching each other and offering healing. As soon as we began, energy flowed through me.

Before I could think, great wings came through my arms and enveloped the lady in front of me. Holding each other's arms now, the energy continued to flow, and I sensed she was really quite ill. The white wings gently embraced her as more and more energy poured in and around her.

"Caroline, thank you. I could feel the energy coming through you." She went on to confirm she was indeed ill and grateful for the healing she received. Others in the room confirmed they saw the angelic presence behind me.

I'm ashamed to remember I was quite blasé at the time. It seemed right that the angels would come through me, and I remembered an experience that happened when I was a kid that left me believing in angels without a doubt.

I stood up, straight as could be, arms in the air and full of reverence. We were practicing for our nativity play, and sunshine streamed through the windows of the hall where we were. I stood there as long as I could, proud as punch.

After a time, I felt faint, and struggled to stay standing for such an important position: I played Archangel Gabriel. Despite my earnest wish to stand tall and proud, the heat of the hall became too much.

I fell to the ground and when I came around, chills ran through my body. It felt so significant. As I share this with you, I feel those same chills.

The angels are real! It's a sign! My seven-year-old self was totally convinced.

Despite feeling so much faith and confidence in the angels at the time, I wouldn't connect with them again until seeing Archangel Michael with my guide, Anna.

After the experience of sharing healing with my new friends, the initial confidence wore off, and I started doubting myself and my visions, and the feeling of the angels faded away once more. I moved through different phases of work and went back to Portugal again, yet it wasn't until moving back to Wales that I was led towards the angels once again.

I started following an online angelic healer, watching her mediations, feeling the energy moving through me when I tuned in, and more and more leaned into spiritual support in my daily life.

After following the healer for a while, I signed up for a call to explore her training course. After an excited exchange of stories, I heard the words I was half dreading:

"Caroline, you're in," her heavy American accent confirmed.

I barely remembered signing up for the call, yet here I was, starting the course. Over the next six months, we practiced connecting to angels, shivers moving through our bodies as we attuned to the energies, seeing visions, and interpreting the messages as they moved through our mind's eye.

My past visions started to make sense, and I got used to calling in the angel's support during my coaching sessions. More and more healings took place as we trusted ourselves and practiced on members of the public.

Despite completing the course and receiving positive feedback, I resisted offering angelic healing outside of my coaching sessions.

All those signs! All those visions, and I still can't offer healing!

It was so frustrating as years went by, and I still had doubts about my connection to the angels, to be known as a healer, and coming out spiritually in the world.

Sure, I was locked up during my psychic awakenings, but that can't be the only reason I have resistance, can it?

Why am I resisting giving healings? I finally cried out to the angels telepathically.

Because you don't feel worthy. You feel like you don't deserve to work as a healer.

But it's so frustrating!

Let us show you why you struggle, I hear them say.

A limp body is in my arms. I'm crying

Fear is running through my veins.

I've killed her.

My heart's sinking.

I'm hiding. Dense undergrowth surrounds me.

They're going to find me. They're going to kill me. I deserve to die. I killed her.

I don't see my death, but I know it happened. I feel it.

Not only did I believe I killed this person, but so did my community. The people I served. The village I served hunted and killed me.

I don't care. I deserved to die. I failed. I failed to help her.

Is it what you really believe? The angels are back, drawing me away from the scene and the images forged in my mind.

Yes. Now I understand why offering healing feels so impossible. In case I fail. In case I kill someone else.

Guilt washes through me, and it all makes sense.

I feel the familiar swirl of energy around me, and sensing the angels again, I let them show me the truth: the lady was destined to die. She was past saving, and the belief that I failed was incorrect. I didn't poison her with herbs; I didn't get it wrong.

It was just bad timing.

Wave after wave of understanding moved through my mind, and I started to see how that lifetime had affected me until this very day.

I stopped giving healing. I was utterly bereft and gave up on myself. Life after life, I felt remorse and went into the shadows. I hated myself.

Yet the knowings were there.

And healing was calling me all along.

Yet I still didn't feel able to offer angel healing—I'd feel responsible again.

Responsible for life and death. The potential for failure, for death, felt all too real.

The huge inner wall that blocked me started to soften. Now I understood what happened all those years ago.

I still don't see why I'm being called to teach about them now.

Why am I anchoring Angelic Vortex Healing? Why me?

The healing modality landed a few years ago in various forms, yet until I was asked to write this chapter, I didn't fully understand its relevance.

I received their insight again in a flash: *You know how to become angelic. You know how to move beyond the limits of your mind, allowing your body to be free. You flow with energy.*

I'm on a busy dance floor, eyes shut, withdrawn from the bustle around me. Rocking and moving with the rhythm, my arms flow in circles. There's no thought here, only music.

Music and me.

I see light in my mind's eye, streams of light moving as I move, flowing as I flow, dancing around me.

Here's my home.

I disappear and become light, dancing with light. The light moves me, and I move the light.

It's bliss here.

Music fills the room, and not one inch escapes. I sense others feeling the music, too, and as we dance, we become one.

We're in the field of music. We *are* the field of music.

The angels bring me back from my memories of dance floors, and I realize how we all move energy; we all work with angelic energies, yet so many of us don't know it.

I ask them for help again. *Help me understand what more I can teach people that isn't already out there. What do I need to know? What do we need to know?*

I still can't see why I'm being called to teach. It feels like a dream that's beyond me.

The angels remind me of times when, despite the guilt and shame I've carried, I acted with love in my heart, wishing to help my fellow brothers and sisters. They show how I side-stepped offering direct healing but took action to help instead.

They tell me every time we act with devotion, honesty, and kindness and speak loving or comforting words, we're activating our own angelic nature. I'm reminded how our chakras are portals to our higher selves.

I realize: *The more we act in alignment with our highest self, the more energy flows through our system.*

They affirm: *This is part of your ascension.*

They carry on with the following examples for us:

• Have you acted with love?

> Then you've aligned with divine love and opened your heart chakra.

• Have you taken action as a result of inspiration?

> Then you've activated your divine service and opened your solar plexus chakra.

• Have you spoken with clarity and honesty?

> Then you're aligned with divine truth, and you've activated your throat chakra.

• Have you sought discernment through contemplation?

> Then you're activating your third eye and aligning with divine wisdom.

• Have you prayed?

> Then you've activated the divine within and opened your crown chakra.

Little by little we're ascending, allowing ever more angelic (or Divine) energy through our system.

Teaching about angelic frequencies means I'm creating channels of learning for myself and others, creating portals of light, and adding to the ever-growing light of the collective.

The first tool below shares how you can call in healing for yourself using the Angelic Vortex Healing method, and the second tool shows you how to tap into angels' wisdom for help in your life.

Angels just *love* to help us with our dilemmas and conflicts, but we must remember to ask. The angels share a message to encourage us to ask:

We're here for you, but ask you must, for we may not, and will not, contravene your free will, for it is your holy right as a divine being.

As I write, they remind me they only bring the answers we're ready to hear, and asking a question means you're opening the door to receive the answer. Many times, we'll hear the voice of our higher self as we align our own wisdom. The energy the angels share allows us to receive revelations all the more easily.

I hope you can see from my journey that no matter how much fear or doubt you may have, you can overcome it, receive wisdom and healing, and move toward the life of your dreams—the life your soul is leading you toward.

THE TOOL

Working with the Angels for Clarity in Your Life

Step 1: Angelic Vortex for personal healing

Get yourself into a comfortable position (lying down or sitting up, your choice). Make sure you won't be disturbed and you're plenty warm enough.

Call in your angels with a prayer:

"Thank you, angels of light, for surrounding me with the colors and energies perfect for me now."

See, feel, sense, or know there's energy swirling around you—your very own Angelic Vortex is around you.

The color or colors you see, feel, sense, or know are exactly perfect for you.

Enjoy for as long as you feel you need to, and when you're ready, bring your awareness back to the room and give thanks to the angels.

Step 2: Angelic Vortex for solutions

Get yourself comfortable once again, and make sure you won't be disturbed.

Think of a challenge you're facing in your life and call in a prayer for the angels to help you:

"Thank you, angels, for helping me find solutions for this challenge (state the challenge)."

Once again, see, feel, sense, or know the angelic energy is swirling around you, and with it, solutions are arising.

You may receive images, thoughts, ideas, or feelings. If you don't receive them at this time, trust they'll come to you when the timing is right.

When you're ready, give thanks to the angels and bring your awareness back to the room

Step 3: Attunement to the Angels

Follow the link to my website below and listen to the audio recording, where you'll receive an attunement to the angels, increasing your capacity to see, feel, sense, and know the angels.

https://www.openlotusliving.com/angelic-vortex-activation

Enjoy your connection with the angels and do reach out to let me know your experiences!

Caroline Mary is a multi-disciplinary healer, life coach, and author. Her specialty is helping people untie the knots of their inner world so they may shine their soul light and live their unique purpose.

Through coaching, healing, wellbeing fairs, and networking meet-ups, she supports people in various ways to unlock their potential and live their best lives. She'll soon be teaching her unique healing modalities to aid the ascension of humanity at this exciting time on Earth.

Caroline enjoys ecstatic dance, singing, and walking in the Welsh countryside. She loves to be near the rivers, lakes, and trees leaning in to their wisdom and healing. She also loves cakes, chocolate, and binge-watching romantic period dramas.

Connect with Caroline:

Website: https://www.openlotusliving.com

Email: carolinemaryandrews@hotmail.com

Facebook: https://www.Facebook.com/CarolineMaryAndrews

CHAPTER 18

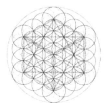

SOUL BLUEPRINT ASCENSION PROCESS

WHO ARE YOU REALLY?
UNDERSTANDING YOUR SOUL JOURNEY

Anita D. Davies

Before reading my story I'd like you to reflect on your life's journey. Ask yourself these questions: What is my purpose? What have my patterns been? What is important to me? Am I happy with my life? Is there something, even if you don't know what it is, nagging at you to find that fulfillment?

MY STORY

He stood opposite me.

He said sternly, "You have a choice, you can go to Italy tomorrow and die, or you can go to the hospital now and live!"

Have you ever had a time when suddenly your path in life changed, and you had no idea at that very point what it would look like in the next 24 hours, let alone in a year?

To understand your soul journey in this lifetime or any other lifetime and what you've come here to learn, you have to understand who you really are and the true meaning of why you had the experiences—good, bad, or indifferent.

This means looking beyond the negative event by looking at what it's showing, teaching, and making you aware of.

The people and experiences you have along the way aren't coincidental.

At the age of sixteen, my life changed forever. I was born with a very rare eye condition, which meant that at age three, I was registered as blind, and up to the age of 16, I attended a school for the blind. I then left home to study at a residential college for the blind for four years (where I met my first husband, the father of my son).

It was also here that I was selected as the first blind woman to join the British Judo Team.

Women at that time weren't allowed to compete in judo at an international level, but this opportunity meant that I traveled the world promoting blind and visually impaired women's judo. I became a World, European, and international champion and ran my own judo club.

I left college, started work, married my first husband, and continued my judo career.

Even though this journey taught me so much, and I experienced so many wonderful things, it was nothing compared to what was to come.

All the changes in my life required me to grow as a person, adapt by learning new skills, and become resilient and resourceful. I was completely unaware of this at the time and for many years.

As I adapted to each new change, a part of me felt that I really needed to understand the path my life had taken me on.

There must be a reason for all the ups and downs.

There must be a reason why I have the ability to not only advocate for and change my life but want to influence those changes for others.

On a soul level, I know each of the people I've met who have been with me—for a reason, season, or forever—are here to play their roles in their soul agreements with my soul, and vice versa.

Before we come into this lifetime, a discussion takes place within our soul chambers with the souls connected to us. We tell our teachers, masters, and guides what we want to learn and experience in this lifetime to evolve.

This is when the other souls in our chamber step forward and take their different roles in our journey based on what we've asked to learn.

Going back to live or die—that was the discussion the night before I left for Italy for my second European Judo Championships for the blind and visually impaired.

I just found out I was pregnant; the concern was that it was an ectopic pregnancy. I was in a huge amount of pain and thought it was because I ate something that didn't agree with me.

Eight months later, I gave birth to my beautiful son, who came into the world with his own physical challenges. This took me down my political path and desire to speak out so he could have the best chance in life to develop to his best ability. I had to fight for everything he needed.

Fast forward eight years, I was pregnant with my daughter and moving through my second divorce.

You know the saying, "The three most stressful things you can do are move house, get divorced, and have a baby?" I did all three at the same time and was experiencing further deterioration of my sight. This is when I noticed patterns emerging.

Things became very challenging and I needed to make choices for my own wellbeing. I was between a rock and a hard place. I knew I had the strength in me to be a single parent again, but it was different now.

The patterns repeated themselves from my first marriage into my second. I ignored all the indicators and told myself a different story.

I told myself, "It must be me; I am the common denominator."

"Maybe this is what love is, and I should be grateful that I have someone to share my life with."

This was compounded by the odd person saying how saintly my husband must be to have to cope with a wife who was blind. This meant I wasn't good enough, and having sight loss meant I was lesser as a person. Therefore, I deserved not to be equal in the relationship. This justified why it was okay for him to lie, be dishonest, and treat me the way he did.

I knew in my heart of hearts that deceit and dishonesty were going on right in front of me.

Discovering I was pregnant with my second child woke me up out of my delusion that this was what I deserved and my low self-esteem. I felt guilty that I allowed my son to witness the trauma of my first, and now my second, marriage. I needed to take responsibility for not just my life but my son's and my unborn child's.

I realized I ignored my intuition because I wanted society's norm of a relationship—the house, the children, a happy marriage, etc. I was willing to do whatever needed to have this.

I wanted love, and I did not want to feel the pain of rejection. Growing up with sight loss in a sighted world meant that from a young age, rejection was something I already felt in many different forms.

I did not want to feel rejected.

I began to realize that trust and honesty were the most important values I held.

As part of my soul journey, I knew I needed to know how it felt to trust and to know when someone was being honest, including my relationship with myself.

Just when you think you're there, another test comes along. This time, I knew I could trust my intuition. This led to the ending of my third relationship but the beginning of my journey of understanding myself, who I really am, and why I'm really here.

I now know this was part of my own journey and my own learning. One of my soul lessons is rejection. To learn what rejection felt like I had to experience it in multiple ways, multiple times.

Choosing the option of being a single parent with limited vision wasn't easy. My biggest challenge was leaving my house and taking my children out. Why?

My son used a wheelchair, and my new baby daughter inherited my eye condition and was sensitive to light. My sight was at a level where I could no longer judge street furniture and people, and I certainly wasn't allowed to drive a car. Getting around meant walking and buses; my parents and immediate family helped whenever they could but couldn't be there every day.

I practiced trusting.

I know a solution will come.

It did.

Three weeks before my daughter was born, I moved into my new house, which was more central to the school, hospital, public transport, and shops. I then discovered an amazing charity that helped resolve the issue of how we'd get about.

A frame was made for my daughter's car seat to slot onto the back of my son's wheelchair, secured with some bungy cord and a sun canopy; we were sorted!

With all of these changes happening at the same time and literally having to do this on my own (as both of my children's fathers were not part of their lives), I had two choices.

You can go to the doctor or you can heal yourself.

I dismissed the idea of the doctor, knowing they'd only offer antidepressants, which I wouldn't take, and chose to heal myself.

I wasn't sure how, but I already started to understand how to trust my instincts and gut feeling; at that same time, someone told me to reach out and grab all opportunities that came my way.

Opportunities are like mystery trips. You never know where they'll take you or what they'll be like, but you have to be willing to seize the moment and trust the journey.

A friend asked me, "Do you want to join me on a crystal therapy course?" I jumped at the chance, trusting it would take me somewhere more positive than I was at that point.

This was the start of my spiritual and energetic journey which led me to the soul work I do today—an 18-year journey of learning different therapies and developing my knowledge and experience in learning and understanding myself, as well as helping others.

On reflection, when I look back at my relationships, I realize that my first relationship was all about my intuition, my second was about my spirituality, and my third was about my realization that in developing my spirituality, I had to discover who I was. These were the amazing gifts these relationships provided.

Have you ever had an inanimate object 'speak' to you?

This was an early experience of my intuition during my first marriage. It involved a letter addressed to my then-husband. Things were hidden from me, and I discovered the truth inside the envelope, which spoke to me.

What I discovered shocked me, and this eventually led to my first divorce.

This revelation and trust in my intuitive guidance grew and has supported me ever since.

This led me further into spiritual development. I've learned to embrace my gifts as a spiritual medium, connect with other people's energies, and be intuitively guided to support and guide healing for others.

My own unique gifts have grown exponentially and have become the bedrock of every aspect of my life, giving me the confidence to develop and adapt my Soul Blueprint Ascension Process.

My sessions with people range from physically touching the place where they experience pain to energetically connecting to them.

I now understand my soul journey, who I am, why I'm here, and who I'm here to help and serve.

I know and understand why I chose to live this lifetime as a soul with sight loss, which makes it easier to deal with and manage the day-to-day frustration of having to interact with the world in a very different way.

THE TOOL

You're about to take a journey with your soul.

- Place your hand on your heart and take three slow breaths. As you breathe in, breathe in love and grace.
- As you breathe out, let go of anything that no longer serves you.
- Let go of any thoughts about what's going to happen after the session.
- Let go of any thoughts about what happened before the session.
- Let go of any thoughts about what someone said or did to you earlier.

This is the time for you to connect to your soul.

- Imagine a golden pyramid above your head.
- Continue to breathe in grace and love, and let go of anything that no longer serves you.
- As you imagine, begin to sense the pyramid above your head.
- Step into this pyramid, and as you step into this golden pyramid of light, take a look around inside.

- In the center of the pyramid, imagine a chair and three levers.
- Take a seat in the chair and look at the levers.
- See yourself pulling on one of these levers.
- When you're ready, pull the lever.

Allow your subconscious mind to connect with your soul and take you to the most relevant timeline for you at this point in time. This timeline could be from this lifetime or any other lifetime.

Feel. Sense that you'll know when you've reached the relevant time line for this session.

Your soul wants to show you an aspect of your soul journey that will resonate with a question you need to understand, an answer you need, or something you need healing for.

- Look around the room.
- You will see a door which will take you out of the pyramid.
- Notice as you step outside—the sounds, smells, and sensations.

These will feel familiar. You don't need to know why at his point. Just notice and remember them.

- Are there people that look familiar to you?
- How are they dressed?
- What are they doing?
- What are you doing, and how do you feel?
- How does the environment look?
- What is going on in that environment?
- Do you feel safe?
- Are you anxious, or do you feel joy, happiness, love, and connection?
- What do you need to understand?

Allow the information to come to you by breathing in love and grace and letting go of anything that no longer serves you.

It's now time to return to the pyramid; when you're ready, select another lever.

As you travel to your next timeline, allow yourself to see, sense, and feel the movement along this journey.

- You notice that there is a platform in front of you.
- You are curious and step out of the pyramid and walk forward.
- As you look down the platform you will see many carriages.

Each carriage represents an aspect of your life, health, wealth, family, community, connection, career, passions, desires, environment, personality, or partners.

- Walk to the carriage that feels like it is the most relevant one for you now.
- Step inside.
- Allow yourself to see, sense, and feel what the carriage is telling you.
- Breathe in love and grace, and let go of anything that does not serve you.
- Allow yourself to know why this carriage is important for you.
- Why have you chosen this carriage?
- What message does the carriage have for you?

It's time to return to the pyramid.

As you sit in front of the levers once more, set the intention that the lever will take you to the timeline where your situation was created.

The timeline will show you how old you were, who you were, where you were, and give you an understanding of what created the situation.

- As you now pull on this lever you'll move to this timeline.

Know that the information you've gathered, sensed, and felt from the other timelines will provide healing, guidance, and the knowing of what to do next and how to move forward with your current situation.

- As you move from the last timeline and re-enter the pyramid, you'll hear a question.

Do you want to release or resolve this situation?

Answer verbally; as you do this, feel the situation change within you, and your soul ascension evolve.

- It's now time to return to the present, to the room you're in.

Allow yourself to know and feel that as you have moved along the timelines, you have received the answers to your questions and the healing required for you to move forward for your highest benefit and for the highest benefit for everyone connected to you.

You can pick up an audio version of my tool at: https://holistic-vision.co.uk/anita_zoom.mp3

Anita D. Davies is an intuitive therapist trained in twelve different energy therapies with 18 years of experience working with people from all over the world, an international speaker, and an activist.

I've worked for over 30 years supporting people with sight loss in the charity sector and, in 2018, was selected as one of Wales's 100 most inspirational women over the last 100 years.

I've received several awards for my work in the community, and for the work I do with women for their personal and professional development.

I'm a director of three community interest companies, which offer services ranging from recycling and repairing things from the home and community to providing inclusive sports and specialized community activities that are inclusive and enable people to connect and grow.

I enjoy participating in a variety of sports, and love cold water swimming and anything that will challenge me, particularly when someone tells me it's something I can't do!

I have a dog named Teacup, and my two amazing children are now adults living their soul journeys. I enjoy meeting with friends for coffee and meals, and will generally try anything once! I love a challenge and the variety my life brings.

The one word people use to describe me is inspirational.

If you'd like some of your burning questions answered or want to investigate your soul journey, email anita@holistic-vision.co.uk or check out my website www.holistic-vision.co.uk

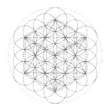

CHAPTER 19

OMNI HEALING

THE WAY TO BLISS,
A TRANSFORMATIVE ENERGY SYSTEM FROM INDIA

Stephanie Jones, Master Healer and Teacher

MY STORY

Angels talk to you when you're out walking. *This place is too big for one person; bring others to experience and teach its beauty.*

This was my first such experience and was the start of my immense, miraculous journey to where I am now.

The fantastic thing is I listened for a change. It was 1998, and I took a walk in the beautiful woods on my country property one day when I was feeling a bit lost and overwhelmed. My husband had a massive inoperable stroke in 1997; I was the primary carer, my family lived far away, and my son was away at university. I was also the main breadwinner and provider and was continuing my successful career at a bank.

The inspiration came to me from my guides to provide a safe haven for others in white-collar jobs and coping with deep, profound challenges and trauma but not knowing where to go. I was to make provisions for informative, stress-releasing workshops in the beautiful countryside I lived in.

Sharing my blessings with others became my main goal—my life purpose. But I didn't know that then.

I planned and created such a place. This was not without difficulties by the local authorities, but eventually, after a year or so of persistence, permission was finally given on Christmas Eve, 1999. Malindi Natural Healing and Teaching Centre was conceived, nurtured, and born in September 2000, and we opened the doors: the new millennium wave of healing would begin. My aspirations, hopes, and dreams were harmonized with the Centre's ideals.

My stars foretold this; my guides spoke.

I attuned to Usui Reiki 1, 2, and Master Healer Teacher in 1997, with credit given to my teacher, Rachael Wilmot, and found it a great start to learning about energy and its capabilities. I learned to trust my intuition and become more sensitive to the mysteries we each hold within us. However, I was looking for more, learning like a sponge through all the excellent teachers from all over the world who came to Malindi Centre. Little did I know I was being primed and fast-tracked to my spiritual home.

In the early days of the Centre, many different therapists and teachers came to work their magic here, and they all sent out emails to their client base to tell of our presence. One person who responded and emailed me from India, Dr. Sameer Kale, expressed his joy at seeing a new healing Centre in the world. It transpired he was a Usui Reiki Grandmaster, an independent teacher of meditation and Yoga. He also told me he recently channeled a new healing system for the world which uses yin and yang energy, with all initiations carrying protective energy to ward off negative energy of any kind.

"Are you interested in me coming to Malindi Centre to teach this?"

After a lot of thought and using my intuition, I decided it was a yes. We went through the immigration system; they were as helpful as they could be. Eventually, he came over from Bhopal in India, where he still lives. I was so pleased to have found him; my life turned around.

During his first visit, I was initiated into levels 1 and 2 of Omni Healing. Learning Sanskrit mantras and symbols was new to me, but I soon got the hang of it. I was struck by the power of the energies and couldn't wait to channel it.

Self-healing is key with this spiritual system, so I used Omni Healing on myself every day as instructed, sometimes more. This ensured I learned the differences between each energy and how it affected my mind, body, and spirit.

Each time it's channeled, Omni Healing works on the human levels of physical, mental, psychological, emotional, auric, spiritual, and karmic. It truly is only when we learn to understand ourselves that we can really help and empathize with others.

After my initiation, I felt immense power while channeling and found I could change not only *my* energy but that of others around me. There was no longer the question, "Which do I use, Reiki or Omni?" It was obvious that Omni was very effective; there was no comparison.

However, running a healing and teaching center alongside my banking career was not, as it turned out, an option. I became very dis-stressed; although I loved my work, it became untenable with increased targets, more hours, and pressure from management above. The Universe took me out of my daily routine and gave me a mystery skin condition on my face and neck. I dealt with this unimaginable horror and challenge, and eventually, in 2004, gave up my bank career and took a massive leap of faith—I ran the Malindi Centre full-time.

I soon found I was only the driver. The Universal energies decided who would come and go to teach or give therapies. Meanwhile, I worked my way up the Omni Healing ladder with Dr. Kale, and by 2001, I was an Omni Master Healer, loving the progress and using more and more powerful energies. I treated people with all sorts of challenges and ailments and had success in turning lives around, providing physical benefits, and allowing their spiritual journey to unfold. Fabulous.

In 2006, I was honored to become an Omni Master Teacher, which gave me a whole new dimension of information and access to the Omni Healing energetic masters and guides. My guru, Dr. Sameer Kale (his spiritual name is Shivananda), has been there to further my journey and enhance my progress. As he always says, "This is your journey; there is no one else, only you." I was initiated into all 17 Omni programs he channeled from Source. Each system delivers new energies to harmonize our human body with the frequency waves of the Universe. We use yin and yang energy, tantra energy, elemental energy, astrological energy, spiritual master energy, crystal and gemstone energy, Rudraksh energy, and advanced Reiki energy.

Since 2001, my own home circumstances have changed quite a lot over time:

- My husband has been through a lot but is still here, benefiting from Omni energy treatments for over 27 years.
- My son is happily married and has his own successful website business. He works from home and has been initiated to the Omni Master Healer level.
- I have two adorable grandchildren who are interested in Omni energy work.
- My family is a tight unit in which we support each other. Omni has facilitated all of this.
- What did I learn over the years?
- I had the strength to hold my own space without feeling guilty.
- Not to be manipulated and taken for granted.
- To detach from all the emotional trauma that engulfed me.
- To voice and further my own goals and dreams.
- That I could enjoy helping others to realize their own spiritual journey.
- Omni Healing benefited everyone who came for treatment, whether it was psychological, mental, emotional, physical, auric, spiritual, or karmic.

Twenty-three years have passed, and I'm honored to teach this fantastic healing system to those who are called to it. During the COVID shutdown in June 2020, I apprenticed with my guru to learn how to expedite distant attunements and organize FaceTime teaching. As a consequence, I'm now able to teach Omni Healing face-to-face and also distantly. What a pleasure to have students from all over the world without moving out of Wales, where I live!

In 2007, I apprenticed to teach Omni Kriya, an energy-based massage therapy, working on the physical, mental, and psychological levels. An exceptional and beneficial light massage, with the client fully clothed, using one Sanskrit mantra and one symbol. I have seen many people benefit from this. In one case, a competitive lady horse rider came to see if we could help. Her doctor gave up on treatment of her back, saying she couldn't ride anymore. We did a course of nine treatments, and she was back in her stables mucking out and back on her horse. She loved riding and was thrilled to be back in the saddle. She even took a second part-time job to help with her finances.

INITIATION TEACHING OF OMNI HEALING

Teaching others is an individual process, and each person has a personalized initiation according to their own energies. The Omni Healing yin and yang energies are introduced into the body through the main seven power chakras (wheels of energy), which are: crown, third eye (forehead), throat, heart, solar plexus, sacral/hara, and root. This energy is then automatically distributed to all 1444 chakras within the body. The root chakra, yin energy, is also initiated to enable spiritual development. At the same time, a positive energy is introduced to protect against all kinds of negative energies, whether intentional or not. Regular channeling ensures this protection is upheld and will grow. Sanskrit mantras and geometrically vibrational symbols are used to human advantage. These are then taught to the student to enable the calling of the energies when required, allowing usage of the type of energy needed in the way taught and stopping the flow when finished. It's so easy, so beneficial, and so life-changing. Support and energetic help are offered to the student as required.

SPIRITUAL PATHWAY

Lots of ideas and information are consistently coming into the physical three-dimensional world to aid our fast-tracking to the celestial levels and beyond to pure Source energy (5D) available to us during these difficult times.

A process of tests and challenges ensures concentration is adhered to and full attention is given to the matter at hand: that is, spiritual purpose and achievement are a priority at any particular time, being the harmonic decision made between soul and Source.

It's important to understand that metaphysically, there is nothing; we are nothing, we have nothing, and yet we create our own daily reality.

How, then, are we destined to live this life?

Being unusually vibrant and learning it's necessary to retain a passionate outlook, being creative in as many frames and levels as possible.

How does all that fit into daily life?

Being nothing does help on some levels as we learn to surrender and let the universal energies decide things. This is all very well, though there is a big 'but'; how do we access the duality within without making some effort? It's not wise to drift along aimlessly, so where is the line?

Source/Soul teaches us to listen to our intuition and gut feelings, upon which we can act out the inspirational thoughts and ideas that come into our heads hundreds of times daily. There needs to be a passion and fire within us to drive the human form forward and to act responsibly to ourselves and our fellow man and woman. This is the duality within us, male and female energies that meld and harmonize our daily lives.

Whatever the demands of your particular work life are, be they working in the caring sector, commercial, corporate, running your own business, or struggling with relationships in your personal life, we can all fall prey to being overwhelmed and eventually to the psychological, mental, emotional distresses which can lead to significant anxieties causing physical and mental challenges and illness.

Omni Healing is a beautiful way to nourish, heal, and protect yourself from the demands of modern life.

There is a massive plus with Omni Healing, which is an accelerated sense of belonging to the Universe, allowing it to flow positively through you and giving you new ways to expand your journey.

Last year, in 2023, a new project came into being called *Retreat into Wellness*, which I am passionate about. This program is coordinated with a friend and colleague, Michael Davies-Eyre, who also has the same heart and enthusiasm for helping others.

We're already running day courses, pamper days, and weekend residential retreats in the UK, and we're planning weeklong retreats in Austria. Watch this space!

Omni Healing:

- Restores physical health, emotional well-being, and imbalances of the mind.

- Aids faster recovery from trauma.

- Supports accelerated spiritual growth.

- Protects from negative energies and intent.

- Balances auric and releases karma-related issues.

- Is used to help others restore their health and well-being.
- Is accredited by the Centre of CPD Excellence, is fully insurable, and carries Continuing Professional Development Points.
- School of Omni UK was formed to support students and give information.
- UK Omni Association was formed to give validity and backing to those practitioners of Omni Healing.

The world needs more healers. If we, as lightworkers, are more grounded, we help not only ourselves but those around us.

Let me help you to be the best you can be, helping you through the anxieties and uncertainties of this year, 2024, and beyond.

THE TOOL

OMNI HEALING MEDITATION

If possible, do this daily or at least once a week for more spiritual awareness and development.

Sit in a chair comfortably with your hands in the open position (palms upward) resting in your lap, shoes off, and feet firmly on the floor. Using a cushion is a good idea to keep feet warmer.

Gently close your eyes. Begin to feel the peace and listen to the noises around you. There may be a clock ticking, a central heating boiler running, others in the room with you, usual sounds in the house, the sounds outside the house. Allow them to fade gently as you connect with the sound and movement of your breath.

Gently become aware of the rise and fall of your chest as you breathe in and out through your nose. Nothing else is important as you begin to connect with your breath. Breathe this way for a few moments (if you're leading this meditation, allow a few moments for the group or person to connect).

Take a few deeper breaths, naturally and without any straining. Feel your cool breath as it enters your nose and your warm breath as it leaves through your nose. Gently breathe in and out. Allow a few moments again for this experience to work through.

See, sense, or feel aware that your breath is now a bright, shining light entering your body and going deeper into your whole body with each breath in and out.

See, sense, or feel the deca-delta light of Omni Healing, a purple light now mixing with the white light and going deep, deep down into your heart and soul.

See, sense, or feel this light spreading through the whole of your head and down your throat into your heart area in the center of your chest.

See, sense, or feel this Omni light as it goes to your solar plexus, your hara (sacral), your root chakra and down both legs, through your knees and into your ankles and the whole of your feet to the tips of your toes.

The light grows stronger with each breath. You can now see, sense, or feel this glow at your heart chakra, and the love it permeates through to your soul and body, refreshing, regenerating, and revitalizing you.

Omni Healing—pure and loving for you.

See, sense, or feel Omni love.

Know this love and pure energy is for your highest good *and* that of others who may come to you. There are no mantras to say, no symbols to see. Just BE.

Allow a few silent minutes to experience this wonderful feeling. This time will grow as you become more used to this energy.

Now, keeping your eyes closed, take a deeper breath, and slowly begin to come back into the room. Realize you're sitting in a chair, hear the noises once more, feel your feet firmly on the ground, and move your toes, ankles, fingers, and hands.

Still keeping your eyes closed, give a little stretch. Place the palms of your hands over your eyes for a few moments, feeling the energy. Then put your hands back into your lap and open your eyes.

You may feel bliss, receive a message from your guides, or be amazed by the mystery inside you.

What a fantastic experience.

Namaste

Born in Austria and brought up in Wales, **Stephanie Jones** is: Master Teacher and healer of Omni Healing, face-to-face and distant Master Teacher and practitioner of Omni Kriya, Energy Massage Therapy.

Master Teacher and practitioner of Usui Reiki. Master Healer of Omni Sutra, Omni Saisutra, Omni Anugrah. Senior Healer of Omni Saitva Teacher and practitioner of Colour Breathing Relaxation system. Practitioner of Omni Shakti, Omni Sphatic (crystal healing), Omni Shiva (Rudraksha Therapy) and EMF Balancing. Practitioner of Omni Vichar, a positive energy using positive intentions. Practitioner of Omni Prabhav, clearing planets' harmful effects on our bodies. Practitioner of Omni Kshitij working on unconscious, subconscious, and superconscious levels, directly working on human behavior. Practitioner of Omni Hast Shastra effective on mental, psychological, emotional, spiritual, auric, and karmic levels using fingers and hands. Practitioner of Omni Shrankhla, effective on the immune system to help Covid symptoms.

Stephanie founded the Malindi Natural Healing and Teaching Centre near Carmarthen in Wales, UK, and is dedicated to teaching others how to live a better life.

She also founded the Omni School of Healing UK and the Omni Association to ensure ethical and energetic continuity and to inform.

"Health and harmony through the natural healing of the body, mind, and spirit."

Stephanie

With gratitude, Stephanie was initiated and guided by Guru Shivananda and Dr. Sameer Kale of Bhopal, India, to promote this unique system.

Stephanie regularly runs teaching, treatments, sends distance healing by request, meditation groups, distant healing groups, relaxation days, retreats, and spiritual courses at Malindi Centre.

Stephanie has three published books:

- *The Road to Bliss: My Journey with Omni Healing*
- *Spiritual Curiosity and Musings with A-Z Guide to Awareness and Spiritual Development*
- *The Things We Say To Each Other*

Connect with Stephanie at:

www.malindi.co.uk

www.omnischooluk.co.uk

www.omnihealingonlinecourses.co.uk

www.retreatintowellness.com

CHAPTER 20

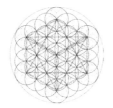

THE DIAMOND CO-CREATIVE SYSTEM®

ENERGIZE. ELEVATE.
EVOLVE INTO LOVE, JOY, AND PROSPERITY!

Amanda Slade, Evolution and Spiritual Catalyst

MY STORY

My Soul got me fired. Up until that day, my life seemed to be going along as I planned.

At forty years old, I lived in a beautiful custom home I built and had my dream job as a Vice President of Marketing and Sales for a publishing firm. Then the call came, "The Tampa office is being shut down and we want you to transfer to New York."

Ten years earlier, I would've jumped at the chance to live in Manhattan. I loved my job. I successfully climbed the corporate ladder in a male-dominated company to Vice President with a staff of fourteen. I worked seventy hours a week and traveled around the country doing everything I 'should' do to be considered a success.

And yet, was I happy? Not really. I had no personal life. I hadn't attracted the love I wanted. I just worked, checking off the shoulds of my career. So, of course, I said yes to the move to New York when I wanted to say no.

I didn't feel empowered to say no because I had no idea what else I'd do. I was in serious debt, needed the paycheck, and didn't believe in myself or trust I could choose something different. The shoulds ruled me.

And my worries, doubts, shame, confusion, and fears ran me:

What if I'm not enough or good enough?

To make it I must work hard, sacrifice, and do, do, do.

I have to prove I'm lovable, worthy, and deserving of all that I want.

The truth was I really had no clue what I wanted. I was lost and could no longer feel or even name my passions. On automatic pilot, I just put one foot in front of the other without really considering the path I took.

So, when the powers that be made their unilateral decision to close the Tampa office without consulting me, I begrudgingly went to New York to keep my job.

On January 2, 1997, my first day in Manhattan, I woke up startled in my hotel room, after having a strange dream. I shook it off and went into the office at 7 a.m. to set-up and get started.

I was the good little soldier who put on the "I got this!" game face. I willed myself to make this work. I began visiting different departments to check on projects. With each check-in, I was increasingly upset. My General Manager undermined everything I implemented and didn't consult me *again* before making changes.

At 11 a.m., we had our weekly phone call. As we began the call, something came over me. I felt a surge of energy flowing through me from the top of my head all the way down my body. This energy took over what I said.

It wasn't me talking; it was my Soul talking and said, "Why are you changing everything I implemented and not talking with me before you do it? I work long and hard for this company and it seems like you don't value my expertise and what I bring to the table. It's so frustrating!"

I took a deep breath and paused to consider what I was saying. But I couldn't stop and continued, "And, why are there executive meetings that I'm not invited to? This is exactly how you treated Gary, edging him out, giving him all the responsibility but no authority to do what he thought best. When I accepted this position, you and I had an agreement that this is *not* how you would treat me, and I would *not* be your puppet. This is *not* what I signed up for. Why in the hell are you moving me to New York when you don't respect me and what I do?"

It was like a cartoon. As the words tumbled out, I tried to gather them and literally stuff them back in my mouth. Interestingly, I stuffed my feelings for eons, so this was nothing new.

It felt like there was another Amanda in the room. This remarkable surge of energy pulsating through me felt amazing; it was so empowering. Knowing what I know now, it was my Soul taking over and saying, "Enough is enough. You're done here, and it's time to move on."

When I hung up the phone, I thought, *well, as a marketer, this is not the way to convince your boss to let me keep my job—I just nailed my coffin shut.* Two hours later, I was called into the CFO's office and fired.

As I walked out of his office, I felt immediate relief like a huge weight was lifted off my shoulders. I thought, *My Soul just got me fired; it has set me free! Thank you!*

I remembered my earlier dream. Its message assured me: *Everything will be okay. It may be rough for a while, but you will emerge with the sun shining brightly upon you.* I had no idea what it meant, but for some reason, I trusted it.

I had no plan B and really didn't know what I wanted for myself. I was well-respected in the industry, so I had many potential opportunities. However, after interviewing for any new marketing job, I always left feeling completely drained. I sat in the parking lot crying and felt defeated. I had no spark or enthusiasm to continue this career path. I knew something had to change, and a new marketing job was not the answer.

I felt immense anger and tumbled into a deep depression. Two months later, I literally fell to my knees in utter despair and asked God for help. And truth be told, I really didn't ask. I *told* God that if things didn't change in six months, I'd be out of here (yes, suicide). I yelled out in hopelessness, sobbing, and hands raised to the heavens, "God, I'm willing to do anything that will help me and my life to change—just show me the way."

Well, what I *didn't* know is that when I did this, I asked to be put on a 'fast track' of healing, transformation, and expansion. I'd been on a spiritual path for years and recently learned about energetic healing. It was now time to get serious about my healing.

I attended workshops, not understanding energetics at all, what chakras were, and how they affected you and your energy bodies, but I knew in my heart that I was in the 'right' place. I had no idea what I was doing, but what I *did* know I always felt better after an energetic healing session.

Getting fired and exploring something unknown was the catalyst for my Soul to take over and show me the way. I had felt dead inside for years, so I knew things had to change if I wanted to live a fulfilling and happy life.

When I started with energetic healing, I became alive again. I could feel energy moving within me. My feelings started surfacing, so I could recognize when something was 'off' for me.

I resisted at first because I feared if I opened the gate to my feelings, I would drown in a flood of emotions and dissolve into nothing. And, for a time, I did.

By dissolving the shoulds, the walls around my heart began to drop. The 'old' thoughts, beliefs, and feelings about who I thought I was and what I should do began to shift. I learned should is really a four-letter word because when we should upon ourselves, we bring ourselves down – it's tied to fear, judgment, and perfectionism.

I was able to let go and tap into the REAL me ...

REAL

Realized Energies Aligned with Love

Did this happen overnight? Not by a long shot.

But my process began to accelerate in 2001 when I channeled in The Diamond Co-Creative System® (the System) with its Diamond Energy Codes and techniques. I discovered how to shift fear and dense, past energetics such as pain, suffering, and struggle into love and the flow of peace, ease, and grace.

The System is a leading-edge alchemical 12th Dimensional technology derived from sacred geometry. The twelfth dimension holds Unity consciousness and the high frequencies of oneness leading you to live and create within the fifth dimension vibrations of love, joy, flow, co-creation, and abundant prosperity.

Each Diamond Energy Code (Code) is designed upon the sacred geometry of Metatron's Cube along with different Universal Light language, symbols, and sound frequencies. This gives each Code specific energetic qualities and purposes. The Codes work within the science *and* the spiritual aspect of the Universe.

Metatron's Cube contains all the sacred geometric shapes of the Divine's creation and represents the patterns of the Universe's construct. The complex structure of Metatron's Cube derives from the ancient configuration of the Flower of Life, which holds the vibrations of Divine love and language of Light.

Love is the energy within the Universe that connects all things. It is considered a strong energy conductor, capable of transcending negative low-frequency energy and attracting positive energies, which tap into higher frequencies and the Infinite.

Sacred geometry is the construct of the Universe—it's the vibrational energetic blueprint for all creation. Its creation is formed through the vibrations of love, which is also the harmonic configuration of your Soul's Divine blueprint.

As a human being, *you* are composed of sacred geometry within your physical structure, cells, and cellular memory. Sacred geometry bridges science and spirituality by bringing spirit and nature together in all life forms.

The System goes to the core origination point and the cellular memory for healing. Unlike other modalities, which may *only* address the symptoms of issues and past pain, the System helps heal and transform from the origination—this lifetime's experiences, past lives, family imprints, or lineage and genetic encodings.

The Codes will move into areas such as your chakras and energy bodies which need assistance at whatever level you require. They each hold a Divine cell consciousness and purpose, so they know what you need and want (even if you don't, especially at a subconscious level). The System will only help create what's in your highest order and infinite potential!

With the System, you can experience immediate and sustainable healings, transformations, and expansions! Plus, the Codes assist you to manifest and evolve into your Soul's greater purpose and plan.

The Codes do not compete with any other modality or spiritual practice. They will only enhance them from the twelfth dimension where 'all is one'!

It was the SOUL-ution I was looking for but didn't know it at the time.

When the System was downloaded to me, I actually rejected it, questioned it, and went kicking and screaming all the way. Why? Well, it meant I would change, and so would my life.

On some level, I liked being in crisis, chaos, drama, victimhood, and confusion. It gave my egoic mind something to do—I created the problem then my ego fixed it. My egoic mind also felt its job was to keep me safe and protected at any cost, including sacrificing my happiness and dreams.

Venturing into the unknown was very scary. At least what I was doing was familiar, even though it was quite uncomfortable.

What was the discomfort? Not knowing what I desired or even liked anymore. I also was ravenous about chasing after the *need* to find my passion and purpose—what was the reason for me being here? I was having financial difficulties and health challenges, too. I was stuck and couldn't see any way out of my circumstances.

All of this was the result of living by my shoulds, which came from what I learned and observed from family and society, conditioning, and programming. I was super co-dependent and wanted everyone to like me, so I fit in. I looked for love, acceptance, and validation from the outside rather than from within. I had huge abandonment, rejection, and victim issues running the show.

I intellectually understood what I believed was 'wrong' with me, but never seemed to be resolved. I cried when I read *Co-Dependent No More* by Melody Beattie. I thought, *I'm such a mess; how am I going to get out of this?* I felt disheartened and forlorn.

What's interesting – everyone thought I had it all together. They saw me as a powerhouse and very successful. On the outside, I looked good, but inside, I was a frightened little girl so worried that they would find out the truth of who I really was.

But who was I really? Up until then, I only identified myself as a Vice President, not as Amanda—a spiritual being having a human experience. And, in that outdated identification, I saw myself as a failure.

I was taught to be who I was by people who didn't know who they were. They lived by their own shoulds, and sacrificed their needs, desires, and dreams to appease others and to try to get what they thought they wanted. There was a right/wrong, good/bad, and successful/failing way of behaving. I became one of them.

I had to get clear on who I was and what I REAL-ly wanted. I had to unearth the dreams that were buried by my shoulds.

THE TOOL

Here's how I did it with the help of the System:

I journaled to tap deep within my Soul.

I quieted my mind and meditated to receive the messages.

I let go and allowed the Universe to show me the way.

But first, I needed to connect with me, my guides, and the Divine.

THE INFINITY BREATH

The purpose of utilizing the Infinity Breath is to help you become connected to you and the infinite possibilities and SOUL-utions that the Universe has for you. This breath connects the spiritual and physical aspects of you and life, so you receive information and steps to take to reach your fullest potential.

It's a beautiful experience to connect before you journal or as you begin your meditation or healing process.

Step 1. Create a sacred space. Light candles, incense, whatever brings you into a quiet state of mind.

Step 2. Close your eyes. Connect with your breath. Invoke a hologram of love to be placed around you and your space.

Step 3. Invite the Divine, your spirit guides, and your Soul's Essence to join you.

Step 4. Set an intention for the time of your journaling, meditation, or healing. Ask for help from your 'etheric team.'

Step 5. Visualize, feel, or sense an infinity sign (a figure '8') that's upright. The top connects to your crown chakra – the top of your head and its center point crosses at the heart chakra with the bottom of the figure '8' connecting at the root chakra – the base of your spine.

Step 6. As you inhale through your mouth (which activates your throat chakra), imagine tracing the figure '8' up from the root, crossing over your heart, to your crown. It doesn't matter which side it begins to go up. As you exhale through your mouth with a relaxed jaw, allow it to drop to the bottom to your root on the opposite side which completes the breath cycle.

Step 7. Repeat this motion of tracing it as you inhale and exhale; this gives your mind a new job by tracing the '8' so it gets out of the way in trying to figure out what's going on.

Let your breath fall into a natural rhythm. Don't push or pull the breath; let it flow naturally. As you continue, the infinity sign may shift position or even multiply; whatever happens, it is in Divine order.

Step 8. Relax your body. Let thoughts and feelings come and go. Just be with the energy and the breath.

Step 9. Give gratitude for what you *do* have, fill your heart with love, and be open to receiving the *more* that wants to come to you.

Step 10. When you feel ready, gently open your eyes, and write down what you have received.

With this connection, **now you're ready to utilize one of the most powerful tools of the System – the Universal Manifestation Template.** It's what changed everything for me!

This tool helps you to:

• Clarify your intentions and tap into your fullest potential.

• Clear energetic blocks that get in your way and keep you stuck.

• Align your energetics so you are a vibrational match to your desires.

The Template helps you save time, money, and energy. I can't tell you how many times it saved me from being distracted by choosing a misaligned path or one that could cause me pain and misery.

The first time I used the Template it proved its weight in gold. I placed a logo on the Template for a new business I was starting. The business was centered around helping healers, teachers, and spiritual leaders to market and expand their reach. Within six weeks, everything about the business and opportunities I had fell away. It was clear that this was not a viable business to help others or sustain myself.

And the message I kept getting as I meditated with or looked at it: *It's time for you to put yourself out there. You're the healer and teacher to market.* Out of this clarification birthed my company, Co-Create Your Success, and we've been serving others for over twenty-three years!

It assists you in discovering and activating your gifts so you can fulfill your Soul's destiny. It ignites a spark within you to become and express your authentic self.

With the System, you can create an abundance of love, joy, passion, flow, and *so much more.* It will Energize, Elevate, and Evolve your life, relationships, health and well-being, financial prosperity, and contribution to the world!

And, because we want to help you too, we're gifting you the Manifestation Template and an e-Book on how to use it so you can Manifest Your ALL!

Download your gift at:

https://cocreateyoursuccess.com/manifestyourallfreegiftforeho2/

When **Amanda Slade**'s Soul got her fired after attaining success as a Vice President of Marketing and Sales for a New York publishing firm and twenty years in corporate, she didn't have a Plan B. *And* she knew something was missing in her life. Amanda took a journey to discover she is an Evolution Catalyst, and with her background, she bridges the 'woo' factor with the practical.

Amanda is the Founder of Co-Create Your Success and Creator of The Diamond Co-Creative System®, which offers Soul-Aligned Possibilities and SOUL-utions. She assists you to identify and claim who you are and emerge as a leader with your unique gifts in your field of passion. Your drive is to make a difference by leaving your legacy to positively influence and impact others as you thrive and prosper in all you are and do.

For over two decades, Amanda has facilitated energetic healing, transformation, and spiritual growth with thousands of clients internationally to help them connect to their Soul's passion, purpose, and plan for life and contribution. She has traveled as far as Australia to teach the System which accelerates Transformation, Alignment, Manifestation, and Expansion to T.A.M.E. your life.

Amanda has been featured on The Shift Network as well as other tele-summits, radio shows, and podcasts. She also speaks at business and spiritual events.

You may be a successful healer, teacher, coach, entrepreneur, or creative who is a change maker, but you want to upgrade and embody a new aspect of your contribution. Or you are struggling on some level, and you're ready to move into what's possible. If so, book a complimentary 20-minute Create Your All! connection with Amanda at: https://live.vcita.com/site/04c0c48a/online-scheduling.

You can add The Diamond Co-Creative System® as a modality to your own healing practice and coaching by receiving accreditation:

https://cocreateyoursuccess.com/diamondcocreativesystemaccreditation/

Connect with Amanda Slade

Email: Amanda@CoCreateYourSuccess.com

Website: https://cocreateyoursuccess.com

Facebook: https://www.facebook.com/cocreateyoursuccess

LinkedIn: www.linkedin.com/in/amandaslade

Subscribe to You Tube: Amanda Slade

CHAPTER 21

DOLPHIN–WHALE ENERGY

A POWERFUL HEALING PARTNERSHIP

Anne Gordon, Walking Whale

MY STORY

I was born from whale.

I didn't always know that. I was the first-born child to middle-class American parents who had no idea how to nurture an infant that fully embodied whale energy, wisdom, and presence. For first-time parents, already nervous about raising a baby, my whale-sized light made them uncomfortable. My mother felt that I didn't need her emotionally and felt rejected, which began a lifetime of resentment, anger, and distance between us.

As I grew up, influenced by the people around me, I forgot about my whaleness, and attempted to live a life as a human. It was not easy. I felt misunderstood, lonely, and isolated. I had a hard time making friends and didn't remember I was a whale in a human body until many years later.

The one thing that always comforted me as a child was being in nature, especially at the sea. We lived on the shores of Puget Sound in Washington State, and my dad had a boat; we spent every summer vacation and many weekends boating. This meant I got to see the orca whales often. Looking back on those magical encounters, I remember the orcas created a feeling of being in the presence of a kind and loving older brother, which brought me a sense of joy and peace.

In college, I studied biology and animal behavior. I worked as a zookeeper, raised and trained wild animals for educational outreach programs, and then trained domestic and wild animals for movies and television for over twenty years.

I had a lot of fun in all those jobs, and the animals I worked with brought me much comfort, but I was still incredibly lonely. I assumed my loneliness was because I was missing an ideal romantic partner. In all of those years, I had a few boyfriends here and there, but never a deep, intimate, long-term relationship.

In 1999 I started feeling the call of the dolphins. I started thinking about them, dreaming of swimming with them, and exploring how to spend time with them. I booked an orca-watching tour to be with them. By then, my father had passed away, and I hadn't been out on the water with the orcas in years.

The tour was incredible. I had found a tour company that used the same make of boat I grew up with, which was now rare because they stopped making them many years before. They even had a boat dog named "Spirit." I knew it was the perfect boat for my reconnection with the orcas.

We headed out keeping our eyes peeled for the telltale black dorsal fins. It wasn't long before the captain got a call on the radio that orcas had been sighted, and we excitedly headed in that direction. Soon, the captain shouted, "Orcas at 12 o'clock!" I saw their familiar spouts and some splashing up ahead, and I was filled with a mix of emotions: joy, comfort, and safety to be in their presence again.

It turns out that not only did we find orcas, we found what is known as a Super Pod. In Puget Sound, there are three resident pods of orcas known as the J, K, and L pods.

A Super Pod is a rare occurrence when all three resident pods get together. It's a celebratory gathering with the whales. There was a lot of excitement amongst the whales. They were breaching (jumping completely out of the water), slapping their tails and fins everywhere we looked.

Our captain maneuvered our boat right into the middle of the Super Pod and turned off the engine. He pulled out a flute and started playing it to thank the whales for gracing us with their presence. The whales reacted to the beautiful music by swimming right next to our boat, turning to make eye contact with us. I was beyond thrilled to look into the eyes of these magnificent beings. There is a powerful, even benevolent depth of wisdom and all-knowingness in their gaze. I still remember that moment clearly after all these years.

It was an amazing day. I was in heaven. I was happier than I had been, maybe in my entire lifetime. I couldn't stop smiling. Everyone on the boat could not stop talking about the incredible experience we had just shared. This magical encounter had reawakened a deep sense of joy within me. It was a celebration of my reconnection with my whale family and my own whaleness.

After that, I read every spiritual dolphin and whale book I found. I meditated with them and felt their presence again in my life which brought me a reassuring sense of peace. I found and attended a school, in Arizona of all places, that taught Dolphin Living Skills and Dolphin Energy Healing.

As an animal trainer, I controlled the animals I worked with. With dolphins and whales, I connected with them spiritually, only occasionally seeing them in the ocean. I realized I had to shift my entire way of being with the animals from control to listening to what they had to teach me. It was more than learning, it was a deep soul remembering.

I learned/remembered that the dolphins and whales are here to show us how to:

- Live in joy and play
- Go with the flow and surf through challenges
- Open to the natural state of abundance
- Live in true unity/community
- Embrace forgiveness
- Find balance and harmony
- Embody unconditional love

And so much more.

After completing 'Dolphin School' in Arizona, I became a certified Dolphin Energy Healer and began giving sessions for friends and clients. I'm not one of those gifted people who can feel or sense energy. When I give a session I feel like I'm doing absolutely nothing but holding space for the dolphins and whales to work through me to send their healing energy to my clients.

In the sessions, even though I felt like I did nothing, I started receiving beautiful visions and profound messages from the dolphins and whales for my clients. At first, there were a few here and there, but as I opened to receive and began to trust the wisdom they shared, it became a steady stream of visions and messages, like watching the most incredible movie in my mind.

What was even more amazing was that even though sometimes the messages made no sense to me, they always resonated with my clients. Even the most off the wall visions—they all made sense to them.

Every bit of wisdom I received, I wrote down, studied, and applied to my own life. I soon realized I was no longer lonely. Even though I lived alone, I always felt the presence of dolphins and whales.

In fact, prior to my reconnection with dolphins and whales, I realized I was terrified of humans. The dolphins gave me a deep sense of peace and confidence in myself, and I realized I didn't need anybody else to live a happy, fulfilled life. I had an entire ocean of spirit dolphins and whales with me everywhere I went. Now, I truly enjoy people and love to connect with them and hear their stories.

The dolphins and whales healed my heart, made me whole again, and brought me back to myself.

It was early in my reconnection with the dolphins and whales that I found myself thinking, *I don't need a romantic relationship to be happy. I am happy. If I never get married, I'm good.*

I lacked nothing in my life.

Within a year, I met and married my soul mate.

Dolphins and whales have lived in harmony and balance with Earth for 30 million years, while humans have only been here for 250 thousand years. We can learn a wealth of wisdom from them.

They taught me a valuable lesson about abundance. Whales represent abundance. They're the largest creatures to have ever lived on Earth, larger than the biggest dinosaurs. They eat the smallest creatures, like plankton, krill, and small fish, and you never see a skinny whale.

In 2005, I was newly married, living in Panama with my husband, who was from an indigenous tribe, the Emberá, who lived deep in the rainforest, only accessible by dugout canoe. It was an amazing experience to be with him and his family, and yet: *How are we going to make money to survive?* The village economy was based on tourism, sharing their culture and history with international tourists.

We lived just outside of Panama City so I could stay in contact with the outside world to be available for any film jobs, either in Panama or back in the US. Panama had an almost non-existent film industry, and being so far away, I wasn't being called for any U.S. jobs. We visited my husband's family's village often, and I enjoyed talking with the tourists there who were fascinated by my unique position and perspective in the tribe, so I thought I could be a tour guide.

I contacted many local tour companies and offered my services as a freelance tour guide. Several of them hired me occasionally. It was fun and paid okay, but it wasn't enough to support us. Sadly, indigenous people are the most discriminated against people around the world, and in Panama, they were often treated very poorly. That meant the only work my husband could find was at less than minimum wage, which was only $15 a day. Not enough to support anyone.

After almost a year of working as a tour guide and struggling to make ends meet, things got extremely tight. One day, after buying one meal to share between us for dinner, I looked at what was left of our money, looked at my husband, and said, "We have eight cents left. What are we going to do?" "Maybe you should go back to California and do some film work," he replied. I was filled with a sinking feeling of fear. There was only one way to find the money to fly back to California, so I sold most of the furniture I brought to Panama with me, including family heirlooms, to buy a plane ticket, and off I went.

I stayed with friends in Los Angeles and looked for work back in the film industry. Turns out I was gone too long—nobody wanted to hire me.

One day, I drove along the coast and looked out and saw some Humpback whales splashing offshore. I stopped to watch them and began thinking about abundance.

In nature, abundance is everywhere. Animals find their food easily and rarely struggle, so why do we humans have such a hard time?

The more I thought, the more ridiculous it felt to me. *Why couldn't I tap into the natural state of abundance.* Then I remembered that whales represent abundance.

As I drove home I continued to think.

Why don't I start my own tour company in Panama that focuses 100% on tours to the village?

I bought the perfect domain name, www.EmberaVillageTours.com, and built a website to promote the tours. Within a week, I started receiving emails from people wanting to book tours with me and sending deposits!

I booked a return flight home to Panama. The tours and customers began flowing in. Websites like Trip Advisor were getting great reviews of my tours, and word-of-mouth referrals kept me extremely busy with my Emberá village tours. Thank you, whales!

Life became easy; money was coming in. I loved my work sharing my Emberá family with tourists. I didn't forget the dolphins and whales. I now lived in a country with two oceans only 50 miles apart.

What species of dolphins and whales can be found here, and how can I get out to see them?

It took me two years to find out that Panama is one of the only places in the world where Humpback whales come to breed and give birth from both the Northern and Southern hemispheres, and nobody was doing whale-watching tours!

Why not me?

It wasn't easy, but I pioneered the whale-watching industry there.

I created a new company, Whale Watching Panama, and offered day tours, which allowed me to spend five days a week during the peak three-month season out on—and sometimes in—the water with the Humpbacks and local dolphins. The beauty was that Humpback season is in the middle of the slowest season for the village tours, so it was a perfect addition to my already thriving business.

While I loved leading the day tours, pardon the pun, I wanted to dive even deeper into connection with the whales and dolphins and my clients to share their spiritual wisdom. That's when I created my Whale and Dolphin Wisdom Retreats, where I took people out to the idyllic Pearl Islands to stay in an ocean-front hotel.

We watched the whales while we ate breakfast! Then we boarded a beautiful catamaran sailboat to spend the day out with the whales every day for a week. It was heaven for me and my clients.

My life was amazing, and the money flowed in easily once I followed the guidance and lessons from the dolphins and whales.

Another profound lesson they taught me was how to dive deep into my emotions when they come up. After 15 years of marriage, my husband made some choices I couldn't live with, so I made the difficult decision to get a divorce. Anyone who's been through a divorce knows the deep sadness that comes from ending a dream, no matter how right the decision is.

As I was separating from my husband, waves of sadness welled up, and I mostly pushed them aside to keep going in my life and business. But one day, while working at home, the sadness was too much, and I remembered a lesson the dolphins had recently taught me—to dive deep into the emotions.

I cleared my calendar for three days, turned off the computer, cried, slept, screamed into my pillow, sulked, and gave myself permission to feel all the pain. It was very uncomfortable, but what amazed me was that on the afternoon of the second day, the intensity of the sadness subsided, and what was left was joy!

When I welcomed the difficult emotions and felt them fully, they didn't last long. I discovered what the dolphins taught me was true: emotions like sadness and happiness are fleeting, yet joy is permanent. It can be easily found when you allow yourself to express emotions as they appear.

This gift of diving deep into my emotions allowed me to navigate my divorce without bitterness and rage toward my husband for his actions. In fact, we went together to sign the final papers and enjoyed our time together despite it being the end of our marriage. We're still good friends and chat often.

During that time, the dolphins and whales found ways to show me they were always with me, even in the middle of losing my human best friend. One day, while I was in a taxi, I fought back tears from the impending divorce, trying to hold them in until I got home. The taxi was stopped at a busy intersection when a city bus crossed in front of us with a life-sized photo of an orca whale on the side!

I felt an immediate wave of comfort and even smiled at how the orcas found a way to remind me of their reassuring presence. The amazing part is

I never saw that bus before and haven't seen it since. In fact, I never saw a bus in Panama with any kind of whale or dolphin on it.

The dolphins and whales continue to share their profound wisdom with me, and my retreats have expanded beyond Panama. Every year, I run my Whale and Dolphin Wisdom Retreats to be with the gray whales in Baja, Mexico, swim with wild dolphins in Bimini, The Bahamas, the humpback whales in Moorea, French Polynesia, and the sperm whales in Dominica.

Recently, the whales came to me one night as I was getting ready for bed: *We want you to start a school.* They guided me to create a Dolphin-Whale Energy Healer Certification course to train and empower others to share their powerful healing energy around the world. It has been amazing to watch others as they open up to their own healing relationship with the dolphins and whales.

I cherish my life of partnership with the dolphins and whales. They guide me, support me, protect me, and love me. They call me Walking Whale. I'm proud to be their ambassador, sharing my whaleness with the human world.

THE TOOL

The beauty of Dolphin-Whale Energy is in its simplicity. There is nothing you have to do or remember.

Ask the dolphins and whales to help you step aside and invite them to use you as a conduit or channel to send their powerful healing energy through you to your friend or client

Tune in and listen with your heart and soul, and be an observer as the dolphins and whales work their magic through you.

I always ask my clients to give permission to the dolphins and whales to adjust their frequencies and physical body in any way that is for their highest good.

You can do this for others, and you can do this for yourself.

Every night before I go to sleep, I say this, "Thank you, dolphins and whales, for sending me your powerful healing energy. I give you complete permission to adjust my frequencies and physical body in any way that is for my highest good." Then I go to sleep and let them immerse me in their healing energy.

I invite you to do the same. You may have dreams with them, or you may not, but never doubt that they're healing your heart and body and gently releasing what no longer serves you.

Dive in and have fun exploring a deep and powerful relationship with the dolphins and whales.

I would like to give you a gift to help you dive into connection with the dolphins: a guided meditation to meet your own personal Dolphin Spirit Guide! Everyone who wants a dolphin spirit guide has one.

Meet your Dolphin Spirit Guide here: www.DolphinSpiritGuide.com.

Anne Gordon has had a fascinating life. She grew up on the shores of Puget Sound in Washington spending time on the water watching orca whales. She studied biology and animal behavior in college and was hired as the first woman zookeeper in the carnivore department at Seattle's Woodland Park Zoo.

She left the zoo because she wanted more interaction with the animals she cared for. She started her own company with a few wild animals, such as a tiger, cougar, wolf, raccoon, etc., taking them out to schools to give educational outreach programs.

She realized that nobody was providing animals for movies and TV in the NW so she began a twenty-year-long career in the film industry training animals for shows like *Homeward Bound, Northern Exposure, Legends of the Fall, Air Buddies*, etc.

In 2004 she moved to Panama to marry a man from the Emberá tribe and began a tour company, Emberá Village Tours to take people to learn the history and culture of her husband's family.

While in Panama she pioneered the whale watching industry and in 2007 created her transformational Whale and Dolphin Wisdom Retreats to deepen her participants spiritual connection with dolphins and whales.

Anne is a certified Dolphin Energy Healer who shares the powerful healing energy, wisdom, and messages of the dolphins and whales with her clients.

She now lives in Southern California just three blocks from the beach and leads her retreats around the world, Bimini, Mexico, Dominica and French Polynesia.

She is excited about her new Whale Wisdom Academy the whales asked her to create to teach a Dolphin-Whale Energy Healer Certification course as well as her popular Pearls of Whale Wisdom course.

Connect with Anne:

Websites: https://www.whaleanddolphinwisdomretreats.com/

https://www.dolphinhealing.net/

Email: Anne@WhaleWisdomRetreats.com

Book a Living the Dolphin Way Discovery Call:

http://SwimWithAnne.com

CLOSING CHAPTER

Each individual is a unique manifestation of divine energy; as such, adopting a uniform approach to well-being is completely inappropriate.

The preceding chapters illustrate the diverse array of healing frequencies and methods available today, showcasing the transformative potential of working with these extraordinary energies, expanding on those presented in Volume I of this book series.

It's essential to recognize that ailments and disharmony can stem from a myriad of factors, often stemming from a combination of sources, such as mental, emotional, or physical trauma, past life or karmic issues, unhealthy lifestyle choices, or exposure to environmental toxins.

The simplest way to visualize this is as an accumulation of energetic disharmony akin to the layers of an onion. A skilled healer can gradually peel away these layers of disharmony to restore balance and alignment across all dimensions of the individual.

The pace of this profound healing journey varies, with some experiencing immediate transformation while others require more time, reflecting the unique levels of disharmony and discomfort within each person. During the healing process, some individuals may undergo a healing crisis on the path to wellness as natural, and vibrational healing methods address the root causes of ailments rather than merely alleviating symptoms.

This process, which often involves purging years of accumulated toxins, stagnant energy, and waste material, can be challenging but ultimately rewarding.

In my personal experience, holistic healing unfolds in harmony with divine timing.

It is essential to recognize the interconnectedness of all individuals on a quantum level. By taking charge of your healing journey, you not only benefit yourself but also the well-being of others you come into contact with, the ripple of healing extends to all that there is. Prioritizing self-care is essential.

The transformative tools generously shared by our esteemed authors can profoundly change your life when consistently applied. All the experts united in this book series agree that empowering you with these tools to initiate your healing voyage is pivotal to your transformation.

The power to unlock these transformative possibilities now rests in your hands; the choice to utilize them is yours to make.

As intimidating as this journey may seem, remember, you are never alone. I urge you, dear reader, to reach out to the expert authors featured in this book. They stand ready to assist you as adept healers, seasoned instructors, coaches, and mentors.

Their guidance is offered with utmost integrity, boundless compassion, and love.

"ARE YOU READY?"

"This is your time – the time of enlightenment.

You can choose, whether to sit, remain in your current position and be blind to the possibilities, or to embrace them.

As always, it is your choice.

The balance of existing in this human world or to soar with all the gifts of your spirit are your choices.

Choose wisely dear ones; your future and indeed the future of all sentient beings depends on this choice".

The Ascended Master St Germain

The Book of Many Colours

Channeled by Angela Orora Medway-Smith, August 2020

RESOURCES

All of the wonderful author tools in this book can be accessed on their respective websites and the links are included at the end of each chapter.

For simplicity, and to help you get the best out of these wonderful Tools, these links are included on a single online web page that you can bookmark on your computer and return to with ease.

Find it here:

https://www.cariadspiritual.com/energy-healers-oracle-volume2-resources

BOUNDLESS GRATITUDE

To each of the amazing healers in both volumes of this book series for sharing your story, wisdom, and light. I feel incredibly blessed to collaborate with these extraordinary humans.

To our publisher, the fabulous Laura Di Franco, and the team at Brave Healer Productions.

To the talented Jenny Hawkyard, the artist whose original artwork graces the cover of this book. Thank you for bringing my vision to life, your image carries such incredible energy, demonstrating the influence of healing frequencies on our beautiful planet and its inhabitants.

To the many spiritual teachers and guides who, from all dimensions over the past forty years, have inspired, challenged, and guided me.

To the thousands of students and clients, I have been blessed to guide and support along their path.

To the dear souls, who throughout my life, have loved, guided, and supported me and helped me learn many lessons.

My gratitude knows no bounds.

OTHER WORK

BY ANGELA ORORA MEDWAY-SMITH

Angela serves the world under the banner of Cariad Spiritual offering:

- Life & Soul Alignment Coaching, bespoke mentoring, Ascension Numerology, channeled readings, healing, and spiritual consultations.
- Cariad Spiritual Academy offers accredited training in intuitive development and energy healing designed to support you to soar.
- Immersive retreat experiences in beautiful, sacred locations worldwide, empowering you with practical tools for spiritual and personal growth in a safe, nurturing space.

Angela is a founder member, and Chair of Divine Energy International a non-profit membership organization, and platform for learning and development for energy healers. Our vision is:

A World Where Divine Energy Is For All.

Find out more at www.divineenergyinternational.org

Angela is a guide and member of Mission on Earth, a sanctuary for souls navigating the profound shifts of consciousness occurring on our planet. Founded on the principles of compassion, community, and holistic healing, Mission on Earth is more than just a support network—it's a beacon of hope for those birthing and embodying the New Earth within themselves. Our vision is:

At Mission on Earth, we envision a world where every individual feels empowered to embrace the New Earth and their personal awakening journey with courage, clarity, and compassion. We believe that by fostering a supportive community and providing access to diverse modalities of healing and growth, we can facilitate personal and collective transformation on a global scale.

Find out more at https://www.missiononearth.org/

Angela has been a world changer with the Wellness Universe since 2015. Our vision:

Global peace by way of happy, healthy, healed human beings.

https://www.thewellnessuniverse.com/world-changers/angelamedway-smith/

"Brothers and sisters, sisters and brothers, we are one, you are one,

aspects, fragments, splinters of Divine Consciousness.

Remember this."

The Seraphim

The Book of Many Colours

Channeled by Angela Orora Medway-Smith, August 2020

SPIRITUAL DEVELOPMENT & WELLNESS BOOKS

The Book of Many Colours: Awaken Your Soul's Purpose With The Divine Rays

The Book of Many Flames: Everyday Alchemy With Esoteric Energies

The Wellness Universe Complete Guide to Self-Care Volume 4: 25 Tools for Goddesses

Strong Mothers: More Than A Survival Guide

Awaken To Your Inner Truth: A Journey of Riches

Love Warriors: The Conscious Expert's Guide to Healing, Joy, And Manifestation

The Energy Healer's Oracle: Tools for Total Transformation Volume I*

High Vibrational Wellness: Intuitive Healing Therapies To Nourish Your Body Temple

All available from Amazon and other online book sellers:

https://www.amazon.com/stores/author/B09L5X6T7X/allbooks

*Rated #21 of the 100 Best Healing Books Of All Time by bookauthority.org

The Divine Rays Oracle Card Deck

https://www.cariadspiritual.com/shop

ABOUT THE AUTHOR

Angela Orora Medway-Smith, "The Practical Mystic," is a Welsh spiritual channel and teacher, master healer, coach, and retreat leader. Her business is called Cariad Spiritual, and she works both in person and online, spreading the light at workshops, festivals, conferences, and retreats worldwide.

Holistic healing is Angela's passion. She's Chair of a non-profit, Divine Energy International, dedicated to promoting energy healing and supporting healers of various modalities and a passionate member of other world changing organizations.

She's set up healing clinics, created charity holistic events and festivals, and trained and supported thousands of individuals worldwide with healing and guidance from spirit.

She devotes her life to awakening divine souls like you to their potential. She believes that we all can transform, emerge from the chrysalis of this human life, 'be the butterfly,' and soar, reclaiming our sovereign self, developing a deep connection to our soul, and aligning with our true destiny.

Angela is incredibly blessed to be a direct channel for the Ascended Master and Angelic Realms. She has published two channeled books: *The Book of Many Colours: Awaken Your Soul's Purpose With The Divine Rays* and *The Book of Many Flames: Everyday Alchemy With Esoteric Energy*.

She's also co-author of six #1 international Amazon best-selling books on holistic healing, all of which you can find here:

https://www.amazon.co.uk/stores/Angela-Orora-Medway-Smith/author/B09L5X6T7X

Angela offers spiritual consultations, coaching, mentoring, retreats, healing, healer, and intuitive development training worldwide.

She loves to empower others to kick-start their healing journey and spiritual development.

When she's not supporting others or with her family, you'll find Angela by water, walking along the banks of the Thames, which flows near her London home, or along the beach close to her hometown in Wales.

Connect with Angela at: https://linktr.ee/angela_orora_medwaysmith

Remember to sign up for her newsletter to receive
monthly gifts and news.

Printed in Great Britain
by Amazon